Praise for Mother's Day Delights
A Collection of Mother's Day Recipes
Cookbook Delights Holiday Series-Book 5

…"If you need that special gift that will delight and honor your mother, *Mother's Day Delights Cookbook* is for you. Inside you will find scrumptious and tantalizing recipes as well as facts, customs, and history about Mother's Day.

The poetry that is included would intrigue and enchant the senses while enjoying the prose with a delicious cup of our blend of Chai Tea featured in *Mother's Day Delights*.

This cookbook truly has something for every Mother, whether your fancy is the distinctive and piquant recipes or the bountiful information and tidbits.

Mother's Day Delights Cookbook will prove to be a treasure in any home and a delightful holiday keepsake for your collection."…

Mary Scripture-Smith
Graphic Designer

…"Mothers have a particularly special place in our hearts. The cookbook *Mother's Day Delights* is a wonderful tribute to the day we set aside to spoil our mothers. Not only does it make an excellent gift itself for any mother, the recipes it contains can be used to create a magnificent feast to celebrate this special day. Especially interesting are the pages in the front of the book dedicated to explaining the history and importance of Mother's Day. The recipes are also easy to follow with numbered step-by-step instructions. That this cookbook is holiday-specific is what makes it unique and desirable."…

Allyson Schnabel
Editor, Teacher

Praise for Mother's Day Delights

A Collection of Mother's Day Recipes
Cookbook Delights Holiday Series-Book 5

..."*Mother's Day Delights Cookbook* is a wonderful expression of love and appreciation. It's an eclectic blend of recipes, poetry, and history, all nestled neatly into one **complete collection**. Instead of taking Mom out to brunch again, honor her with something deliciously different. *Mother's Day Delights* is a gift that she can enjoy all year long!"...

Kimberly Carter
Publicist

..."Mother's day is a great time not just to celebrate motherhood, but to bring the family together, and what better way to do so than to make a home cooked meal.

Mother's Day Delights Cookbook is just the tool you need for that purpose. It is a gift that continues to remain fresh and new each time you pull it out. There are hundreds of recipes with a large range of choices that will please any palate.

The great thing about this cookbook is that it doesn't end there. This book has it all covered. Whether sitting in front of a fire with a cup of tea reading the poetry or making your own jams and jellies, this book can be your guide. With plenty of pleasant reading and recipes that cover appetizers to wines and spirits your will be sure to find that this is one book that stays on the counter and out of the cupboard.

Whether you buy it for yourself or as a gift, you are sure to be rewarded with satisfied smiles from the ones you love."...

Ed Archambeault
Spokane, WA

Praise for Mother's Day Delights
A Collection of Mother's Day Recipes
Cookbook Delights Holiday Series-Book 5

…"*Mother's Day Delights Cookbook* is not only a cookbook but a wealth of information about Mother's Day. It includes fascinating facts, the history of Mother's Day, quotes, poetry, and more. It even includes information on Mother's Day celebrations around the world.

In addition to all of this information, it has a collection of over 250 delicious recipes that will be enjoyed by your mom, family, and friends.

This is a great value for the price and makes a wonderful gift."…

Dr. James G. Hood
Editor

…"Whether you are looking for a special gift for Mother's Day or would like to dazzle your mother with a delicious meal, *Mother's Day Delights Cookbook* is the perfect choice. Packed with recipes, insightful poetry, and information about the holiday, this cookbook is a treasure-trove of inspiration. Many of the recipes are easy enough that the kids can help Dad out in the kitchen to make a special breakfast in bed, and some are even suitable for older children to make it on their own."…

Kim Saunders

Mother's Day Delights

A Collection of Mother's Day Recipes
Cookbook Delights Holiday Series-Book 5

Karen Jean Matsko Hood

Current and Future Cookbooks
By Karen Jean Matsko Hood

DELIGHTS SERIES

Almond Delights
Anchovy Delights
Apple Delights
Apricot Delights
Artichoke Delights
Asparagus Delights
Avocado Delights
Banana Delights
Barley Delights
Basil Delights
Bean Delights
Beef Delights
Beer Delights
Beet Delights
Blackberry Delights
Blueberry Delights
Bok Choy Delights
Boysenberry Delights
Brazil Nut Delights
Broccoli Delights
Brussels Sprouts Delights
Buffalo Berry Delights
Butter Delights
Buttermilk Delights
Cabbage Delights
Calamari Delights
Cantaloupe Delights
Caper Delights
Cardamom Delights
Carrot Delights
Cashew Delights
Cauliflower Delights
Celery Delights
Cheese Delights
Cherry Delights
Chestnut Delights
Chicken Delights
Chili Pepper Delights
Chive Delights

Chocolate Delights
Chokecherry Delights
Cilantro Delights
Cinnamon Delights
Clam Delights
Clementine Delights
Coconut Delights
Coffee Delights
Conch Delights
Corn Delights
Cottage Cheese Delights
Crab Delights
Cranberry Delights
Cucumber Delights
Cumin Delights
Curry Delights
Date Delights
Edamame Delights
Egg Delights
Eggplant Delights
Elderberry Delights
Endive Delights
Fennel Delights
Fig Delights
Filbert (Hazelnut) Delights
Fish Delights
Garlic Delights
Ginger Delights
Ginseng Delights
Goji Berry Delights
Grape Delights
Grapefruit Delights
Grapple Delights
Guava Delights
Ham Delights
Hamburger Delights
Herb Delights
Herbal Tea Delights
Honey Delights
Honeyberry Delights

Honeydew Delights
Horseradish Delights
Huckleberry Delights
Jalapeño Delights
Jerusalem Artichoke Delights
Jicama Delights
Kale Delights
Kiwi Delights
Kohlrabi Delights
Lavender Delights
Leek Delights
Lemon Delights
Lentil Delights
Lettuce Delights
Lime Delights
Lingonberry Delights
Lobster Delights
Loganberry Delights
Macadamia Nut Delights
Mango Delights
Marionberry Delights
Milk Delights
Mint Delights
Miso Delights
Mushroom Delights
Mussel Delights
Nectarine Delights
Oatmeal Delights
Olive Delights
Onion Delights
Orange Delights
Oregon Berry Delights
Oyster Delights
Papaya Delights
Parsley Delights
Parsnip Delights
Pea Delights
Peach Delights
Peanut Delights
Pear Delights
Pecan Delights
Pepper Delights
Persimmon Delights
Pine Nut Delights
Pineapple Delights

Pistachio Delights
Plum Delights
Pomegranate Delights
Pomelo Delights
Popcorn Delights
Poppy Seed Delights
Pork Delights
Potato Delights
Prickly Pear Cactus Delights
Prune Delights
Pumpkin Delights
Quince Delights
Quinoa Delights
Radish Delights
Raisin Delights
Raspberry Delights
Rhubarb Delights
Rice Delights
Rose Delights
Rosemary Delights
Rutabaga Delights
Salmon Delights
Salmonberry Delights
Salsify Delights
Savory Delights
Scallop Delights
Seaweed Delights
Serviceberry Delights
Sesame Delights
Shallot Delights
Shrimp Delights
Soybean Delights
Spinach Delights
Squash Delights
Star Fruit Delights
Strawberry Delights
Sunflower Seed Delights
Sweet Potato Delights
Swiss Chard Delights
Tangerine Delights
Tapioca Delights
Tayberry Delights
Tea Delights
Teaberry Delights
Thimbleberry Delights

Tofu Delights
Tomatillo Delights
Tomato Delights
Trout Delights
Truffle Delights
Tuna Delights
Turkey Delights
Turmeric Delights
Turnip Delights
Vanilla Delights
Walnut Delights
Wasabi Delights
Watermelon Delights
Wheat Delights
Wild Rice Delights
Yam Delights
Yogurt Delights
Zucchini Delights

CITY DELIGHTS
Chicago Delights
Coeur d'Alene Delights
Great Falls Delights
Honolulu Delights
Minneapolis Delights
Phoenix Delights
Portland Delights
Sandpoint Delights
Scottsdale Delights
Seattle Delights
Spokane Delights
St. Cloud Delights

FOSTER CARE
Foster Children Cookbook
  and Activity Book
Foster Children's Favorite
  Recipes
Holiday Cookbook for
  Foster Families

GENERAL THEME
  DELIGHTS
Appetizer Delights
Baby Food Delights
Barbeque Delights

Beer-Making Delights
Beverage Delights
Biscotti Delights
Bisque Delights
Blender Delights
Bread Delights
Bread Maker Delights
Breakfast Delights
Brunch Delights
Cake Delights
Campfire Food Delights
Candy Delights
Canned Food Delights
Cast Iron Delights
Cheesecake Delights
Chili Delights
Chowder Delights
Cocktail Delights
College Cooking Delights
Comfort Food Delights
Cookie Delights
Cooking for One Delights
Cooking for Two Delights
Cracker Delights
Crepe Delights
Crockpot Delights
Dairy Delights
Dehydrated Food Delights
Dessert Delights
Dinner Delights
Dutch Oven Delights
Foil Delights
Fondue Delights
Food Processor Delights
Fried Food Delights
Frozen Food Delights
Fruit Delights
Gelatin Delights
Grilled Delights
Hiking Food Delights
Ice Cream Delights
Juice Delights
Kid's Delights
Kosher Diet Delights
Liqueur-Making Delights

8

Liqueurs and Spirits Delights
Lunch Delights
Marinade Delights
Microwave Delights
Milk Shake and Malt Delights
Panini Delights
Pasta Delights
Pesto Delights
Phyllo Delights
Pickled Food Delights
Picnic Food Delights
Pizza Delights
Preserved Delights
Pudding and Custard Delights
Quiche Delights
Quick Mix Delights
Rainbow Delights
Salad Delights
Salsa Delights
Sandwich Delights
Sea Vegetable Delights
Seafood Delights
Smoothie Delights
Snack Delights
Soup Delights
Supper Delights
Tart Delights
Torte Delights
Tropical Delights
Vegan Delights
Vegetable Delights
Vegetarian Delights
Vinegar Delights
Wildflower Delights
Wine Delights
Winemaking Delights
Wok Delights

GIFTS-IN-A-JAR SERIES
Beverage Gifts-in-a-Jar
Christmas Gifts-in-a-Jar
Cookie Gifts-in-a-Jar
Gifts-in-a-Jar
Gifts-in-a-Jar Catholic
Gifts-in-a-Jar Christian

Holiday Gifts-in-a-Jar
Soup Gifts-in-a-Jar

HEALTH-RELATED DELIGHTS
Achalasia Diet Delights
Adrenal Health Diet Delights
Anti-Acid Reflux Diet Delights
Anti-Cancer Diet Delights
Anti-Inflammation Diet
  Delights
Anti-Stress Diet Delights
Arthritis Delights
Bone Health Diet Delights
Diabetic Diet Delights
Diet for Pink Delights
Fibromyalgia Diet Delights
Gluten-Free Diet Delights
Healthy Breath Diet Delights
Healthy Digestion Diet
  Delights
Healthy Heart Diet Delights
Healthy Skin Diet Delights
Healthy Teeth Diet Delights
High-Fiber Diet Delights
High-Iodine Diet Delights
High-Protein Diet Delights
Immune Health Diet Delights
Kidney Health Diet Delights
Lactose-Free Diet Delights
Liquid Diet Delights
Liver Health Diet Delights
Low-Calorie Diet Delights
Low-Carb Diet Delights
Low-Fat Diet Delights
Low-Sodium Diet Delights
Low-Sugar Diet Delights
Lymphoma Health Support
  Diet Delights
Multiple Sclerosis Healthy
  Diet Delights
No Flour No Sugar Diet
  Delights
Organic Food Delights
pH-Friendly Diet Delights

Pregnancy Diet Delights
Raw Food Diet Delights
Sjögren's Syndrome Diet
  Delights
Soft Food Diet Delights
Thyroid Health Diet Delights

HOLIDAY DELIGHTS
Christmas Delights
Easter Delights
Father's Day Delights
Fourth of July Delights
Grandparent's Day Delights
Halloween Delights
Hanukkah Delights
Labor Day Weekend Delights
Memorial Day Weekend
  Delights
Mother's Day Delights
New Year's Delights
St. Patrick's Day Delights
Thanksgiving Delights
Valentine Delights

HOOD AND MATSKO
  FAMILY FAVORITES
Hood and Matsko Family
  Appetizers Cookbook
Hood and Matsko Family
  Beverages Cookbook
Hood and Matsko Family
  Breads and Rolls Cookbook
Hood and Matsko Family
  Breakfasts Cookbook
Hood and Matsko Family
  Cakes Cookbook
Hood and Matsko Family
  Candies Cookbook
Hood and Matsko Family
  Casseroles Cookbook
Hood and Matsko Family
  Cookies Cookbook
Hood and Matsko Family
  Desserts Cookbook
Hood and Matsko Family

Dressings, Sauces, and
  Condiments Cookbook
Hood and Matsko Family
  Ethnic Cookbook
Hood and Matsko Family
  Jams, Jellies, Syrups,
  Preserves, and Conserves
Hood and Matsko Family
  Main Dishes Cookbook
Hood and Matsko Family,
  Pies Cookbook
Hood and Matsko Family
  Preserving Cookbook
Hood and Matsko Family
  Salads and Salad Dressings
Hood and Matsko Family
  Side Dishes Cookbook
Hood and Matsko Family
  Vegetable Cookbook
Hood and Matsko Family,
  Aunt Katherine's Recipe
  Collection, Vol. I-II
Hood and Matsko Family,
  Grandma Bert's Recipe
  Collection, Vol. I-IV

HOOD AND MATSKO
  FAMILY HOLIDAY
Hood and Matsko Family
  Favorite Birthday Recipes
Hood and Matsko Family
  Favorite Christmas Recipes
Hood and Matsko Family
  Favorite Christmas Sweets
Hood and Matsko Family
  Easter Cookbook
Hood and Matsko Family
  Favorite Thanksgiving Recipes

INTERNATIONAL
  DELIGHTS
African Delights
African American Delights
Australian Delights
Austrian Delights

Brazilian Delights
Canadian Delights
Chilean Delights
Chinese Delights
Czechoslovakian Delights
English Delights
Ethiopian Delights
Fijian Delights
French Delights
German Delights
Greek Delights
Hungarian Delights
Icelandic Delights
Indian Delights
Irish Delights
Italian Delights
Korean Delights
Mexican Delights
Native American Delights
Polish Delights
Russian Delights
Scottish Delights
Slovenian Delights
Swedish Delights
Thai Delights
The Netherlands Delights
Yugoslavian Delights
Zambian Delights

REGIONAL DELIGHTS
Glacier National Park Delights
Northwest Regional Delights
Oregon Coast Delights
Schweitzer Mountain Delights
Southwest Regional Delights
Tropical Delights
Washington Wine Country
  Delights
Wine Delights of Walla
  Walla Wineries
Yellowstone National Park
  Delights

SEASONAL DELIGHTS
Autumn Harvest Delights

Spring Harvest Delights
Summer Harvest Delights
Winter Harvest Delights

SPECIAL EVENTS
  DELIGHTS
Birthday Delights
Coffee Klatch Delights
Super Bowl Delights
Tea Time Delights

STATE DELIGHTS
Alaska Delights
Arizona Delights
Georgia Delights
Hawaii Delights
Idaho Delights
Illinois Delights
Iowa Delights
Louisiana Delights
Minnesota Delights
Montana Delights
North Dakota Delights
Oregon Delights
South Dakota Delights
Texas Delights
Washington Delights

U.S. TERRITORIES
  DELIGHTS
Cruzan Delights
U.S. Virgin Island Delights

MISCELLANEOUS
  COOKBOOKS
Getaway Studio Cookbook
The Soup Doctor's Cookbook

BILINGUAL DELIGHTS
  SERIES
Apple Delights, English-
  French Edition
Apple Delights, English-
  Russian Edition
Apple Delights, English-
  Spanish Edition

Huckleberry Delights,
English-French Edition
Huckleberry Delights,
English-Russian Edition
Huckleberry Delights,
English-Spanish Edition

CATHOLIC DELIGHTS SERIES
Apple Delights Catholic
Coffee Delights Catholic
Easter Delights Catholic
Huckleberry Delights Catholic
Tea Delights Catholic

CATHOLIC BILINGUAL DELIGHTS SERIES
Apple Delights Catholic,
English-French Edition
Apple Delights Catholic,
English-Russian Edition
Apple Delights Catholic,
English-Spanish Edition
Huckleberry Delights
Catholic, English-Spanish
Edition

CHRISTIAN DELIGHTS SERIES
Apple Delights Christian
Coffee Delights Christian
Easter Delights Christian
Huckleberry Delights Christian
Tea Delights Christian

CHRISTIAN BILINGUAL DELIGHTS SERIES
Apple Delights Christian,
English-French Edition
Apple Delights Christian,
English-Russian Edition
Apple Delights Christian,
English-Spanish Edition
Huckleberry Delights
Christian, English-Spanish
Edition

FUNDRAISING COOKBOOKS
Ask about our fundraising
cookbooks to help raise
funds for your organization.

The above books are also available in bilingual versions. Please contact Whispering Pine Press International, Inc., for details.

Please note that some books are future books and are currently in production. Please contact us for availability date. Prices are subject to change without notice.

The above list of books is not all-inclusive. For a complete list please visit our website or contact us at:

Whispering Pine Press International, Inc.
Your Northwest Book Publishing Company
P.O. Box 214
Spokane Valley, WA 99037-0214 USA
Phone: (509) 928-8700 | Fax: (509) 922-9949
Email: sales@WhisperingPinePress.com
Publisher Websites: www.WhisperingPinePress.com
www.WhisperingPinePressBookstore.com
Blog: www.WhisperingPinePressBlog.com

Mother's Day Delights

A Collection of Mother's Day Recipes
Cookbook Delights Holiday Series-Book 5

Karen Jean Matsko Hood

Published by:

Whispering Pine Press International, Inc.
Your Northwest Book Publishing Company

P.O. Box 214
Spokane Valley, WA 99037-0214 USA
Phone: (509) 928-8700 | Fax: (509) 922-9949
Email: sales@WhisperingPinePress.com
Websites: www.WhisperingPinePress.com
www.WhisperingPinePressBookstore.com
Blog: www.WhisperingPinePressBlog.com
SAN 253-200X
Printed in the U.S.A.

Published by Whispering Pine Press International, Inc.
P.O. Box 214
Spokane Valley, Washington 99037-0214 USA

For sales outside the United States, please contact the Whispering Pine Press International, Inc., International Sales Department.

Manufactured in the United States of America. This paper is acid-free and 100% chlorine free.

Book and Cover Design by Artistic Design Service, Inc.
P. O. Box 1782
Spokane Valley, WA 99037-1792 USA
www.ArtisticDesignService.com

Library of Congress Number (LCCN): 2014901413

Hood, Karen Jean Matsko
    Title: Mother's Day Delights Cookbook: A Collection of Mother's Day Recipes: Cookbook Delights Holiday Series-Book 5

    p.   cm.

ISBN: 978-1-59434-374-2   case bound
ISBN: 978-1-59434-376-6   perfect bound
ISBN: 978-1-59434-375-9   spiral bound
ISBN: 978-1-59434-377-3   comb bound
ISBN: 978-1-59434-379-7   E-PDF
ISBN: 978-1-59210-427-7   E-PUB
ISBN: 978-1-59434-378-0   E-PRC

First Edition: January 2014
1. Cookery *(Mother's Day Cookbook: A Collection of Mother's Day Recipes: Cookbook Delights Holiday Series-Book 5)* 1. Title

Mother's Day Delights Cookbook
A Collection of Mother's Day Recipes
Cookbook Delights Holiday Series-Book 5

Gift Inscription

To: _____

From: _____

Date: _____

Special Message: _____

_____

_____

_____

_____

_____

_____

_____

*It is always nice to receive a personal note to
create a special memory.*

www.MothersDayDelights.com
www.WhisperingPinePress.com
www.WhisperingPinePressBookstore.com

Dedications

To my husband and best friend, Jim.

To our seventeen children: Gabriel, Brianne Kristina and her husband Moulik Kothari, Marissa Kimberly, Janelle Karina and her husband Paul Turcotte, Mikayla Karlene, Kyler James, Kelsey Katrina, Corbin Joel, Caleb Jerome, Keisha Kalani Hiwot, Devontay Joshua, Kianna Karielle Selam, Rosy Kiara, Mercedes Katherine, Jasmine Khalia Wengel, Cheyenne Krystal, and Annalise Kaylee Marie.

To our grandchild Nola Paige and our future grandchildren.

To our foster grandchild, Courtney, Lorenzo, and Leah.

To my brother, Stephen, and his wife, Karen.

To my husband's ten siblings: Gary, Colleen, John, Dan, Mary, Ray, Ann, Teresa, Barbara, Agnes, and their families.

In loving memory of my mom, who passed away in 2007; my dad, who passed away in 1976; and my sister, Sandy, who passed away due to multiple sclerosis in 1999.

To Sandy's three sons: Monte, Bradley, and Derek. To Monte's wife, Sarah, and their children: Liam, Alice, Charlie, and Samuel and their foster children. To Bradley's wife, Shawnda, and their children: Anton, Isaac, and Isabel.

To our foster children past and present: Krystal, Sara, Rebecca, Janice, Devontay Joshua, Mercedes Katherine, Zha'Nell, Makia, Onna, Cheyenne Krystal, Onna Marie, Nevaeh, and Zada, our future foster children, and all foster children everywhere.

To the Court Appointed Special Advocate (CASA) Volunteer Program in the judicial system which benefits abused and neglected children.

To the Literacy Campaign dedicated to promoting literacy throughout the world.

Acknowledgements

The author would like to acknowledge all those individuals who helped me during my time in writing this book. Appreciation is extended for all their support and effort they put into this project.

Deep gratitude and profound thanks are owed to my husband, Jim, for giving freely of his time and encouragement during this project.

Thanks are owed to my children Gabriel, Brianne Kristina and her husband Moulik Kothari, Marissa Kimberly, Janelle Karina and her husband Paul Turcotte, Mikayla Karlene, Kyler James, Kelsey Katrina, Corbin Joel, Caleb Jerome, Keisha Kalani Hiwot, Devontay Joshua, Kianna Karielle Selam, Rosy Kiara, Mercedes Katherine, Jasmine Khalia Wengel, Cheyenne Krystal, and Annalise Kaylee Marie. All of these persons inspire my writing.

Thanks are due to Teresa L. Allen and Sharron Thompson for their assistance in typing this manuscript for publication. Thanks go to Artistic Design Service, Inc. for their assistance in formatting and providing a graphic design of this manuscript for publication. This project could not have been completed without them.

Many thanks are due to members of my family, all of whom were very supportive during the time it took to complete this project. Their patience and support are greatly appreciated.

Mother's Day Delights Cookbook
Table of Contents

Mother's Day Delights Cookbook
A Collection of Mother's Day Recipes
Cookbook Delights Holiday Series-Book 5

Introduction

Mother's Day Delights Cookbook is the perfect gift for Mom or anyone who wishes to make this Mother's Day unforgettable. The recipes in this book have been collected around the themes, colors, and symbols of this special day to help readers honor and celebrate mothers everywhere on Mother's Day or any other day, as well.

As a poet, I found it enjoyable to color this cookbook with poetry so that readers could savor the metaphorical richness of this special day for mothers. Also included are some articles on history, cultivation, and botanical information, along with interesting facts about Mother's Day. Sections that discuss health and nutrition as well as some information on Mother's Day celebrations are also included in this book.

The *Cookbook Delights Series* would not be complete without *Mother's Day Delights Cookbook*. We hope you enjoy reading this cookbook as well as trying out all of the delicious recipes that have been gathered together for your culinary adventures.

The cookbook is organized in convenient alphabetical sections to assist you in finding recipes related to the type of cooking you need: appetizers and dips; beverages; breads and rolls; breakfasts; cakes; candies; cookies; desserts; dressings, sauces, and condiments; jams, jellies, and syrups; main dishes; pies; preserving; salads; side dishes; soups; and wines and spirits.

Following is a collection of information and recipes gathered and modified to bring you *Mother's Day Delights Cookbook: A Collection of Mother's Day Recipes, Cookbook Delights Series* by Karen Jean Matsko Hood.

Mother's Day Delights Cookbook
A Collection of Mother's Day Recipes
Cookbook Delights Holiday Series-Book 5

Mother's Day Botanical Classification

Mother's Day Botanical Classification

The *Caryophyllaceae*, the pink or carnation family, are a family of dicotyledons, flowering plants, included in the order *Caryophyllales*. This is a large family with 88 genera and some 2,000 species.

The carnation (*Dianthus caryophyllus*) is a flowering plant native to the Near East and has been cultivated for the last 2,000 years. Its original natural flower color was pink-hued, but later, cultivars of other colors, including red, white, yellow, and green, have been developed. Although originally applied to the species *Dianthus caryophyllus*, the name Carnation is also often applied to some of the other species of *Dianthus*, and more particularly to garden hybrids between *D. caryophyllus* and other species in the genus.

This is a cosmopolitan family of herbaceous plants from temperate climates. A few grow on tropical mountains. carnations, firepink, and campion are representative members. Many species are grown as ornamental plants, but some are widespread weeds. Most species grow in the Mediterranean and bordering regions of Europe and Asia. The number of genera and species in the southern hemisphere is rather small.

Despite its size and the somewhat doubtful mutual relationships, this family is rather uniform and easily recognizable. Most are herbacaceous annuals or perennials, dying off above ground each year.

Mother's Day Delights Cookbook
A Collection of Mother's Day Recipes
Cookbook Delights Holiday Series-Book 5

Mother's Day Celebrations

Mother's Day Celebrations

In most countries, Mother's Day is a new concept copied from western civilization. In many African countries, Mother's Day takes its origins from the British concept of Mother's Day. In most of East Asia, Mother's Day is a heavily marketed and commercialized concept copied straight from Mother's Day in the USA.

Mothering Sunday in the United Kingdom falls on the fourth Sunday of Lent (typically March or early April); it is commonly called "Mother's Day" but has no direct connection to the American practice. It is believed to have originated from the Christian practice of visiting ones mother church annually, this meant that most familes would be reunited on this day. Most historians believe that young apprentices and young women in servitude were released by their masters that weekend in order to visit their families.

Mother's Day is celebrated on various days of the year in different countries because they have a number of different origins. One school of thought claims this day emerged from a custom of mother worship in ancient Greece. Mother worship — which kept a festival to Cybele, a great mother of gods, and Rhea, the wife of Cronus — was held on March 15 to March 18 around Asia Minor.

Mother's Day is now celebrated in many countries around the world. Australia, Mexico, Denmark, Finland, Italy, Turkey, Belgium, Russia, China, Thailand, all have special celebrations to honor Mothers, but not in the same way or on the same day as the United States.

Mother's Day Delights Cookbook
A Collection of Mother's Day Recipes
Cookbook Delights Holiday Series-Book 5

Mother's Day Cultivation and Gardening

Mother's Day Cultivation and Gardening

Carnations grow readily from cuttings made of the suckers that form around the base of the stem, the side shoots of the flowering stem, or the main shoots before they show flower-buds. The cuttings from the base make the best plants in most cases. These cuttings may be taken from a plant at any time through the fall or winter, rooted in sand and potted up, to be held in pots until the planting out time in the spring, usually in April, or any time when the ground is ready to handle. Care should be taken to pinch out the tops of the young plants while growing in the pot, and later while in the ground, causing them to grow stocky and send out new growths along the stem. The young plants should be grown cool, a temperature of 45 degrees F. suiting them well. Attention should be given to spraying the cuttings each day while in the house to keep down the red spider, which is very partial to the carnation.

In the summer, the plants are grown in the field, and not in pots, being transplanted from the cutting-box. The soil in which they are to be planted should be moderately rich and loose. Clean cultivation should be given throughout the summer. Frequently pinch out the tops.

The plants are taken up in September and potted firmly, and well watered; then set in a cool, partially shaded situation until root growth has started, and watering the plant as it shows need of water.

Mother's Day Delights Cookbook
A Collection of Mother's Day Recipes
Cookbook Delights Holiday Series-Book 5

Mother's Day Facts

Mother's Day Facts

Chinese family names are often formed (begin) with a sign that means "mother." It's a nice way of honoring their mom's long past.

Japan's Imperial family traces their descent from Omikami Amaterasu, the Mother of the World.

Hindu scripture credits the Great Mother, Kali Ma, with the invention of writing through alphabets, pictographs, and beautiful sacred images.

Native American Indian women have long been honored with the name, "Life of the Nation" for their gift of motherhood to the tribes.

In the Bible, Eve is credited with being the "Mother of All the Living."

Mother Earth is also known as "Terra Firma." That title is a Latin translation of some lines from one of the Greek poet, Homer's, greatest poems.

Eighty-one percent of women 40 to 44 years old are mothers. In 1980, ninety percent of women in that age group were mothers.

Buddha honored mothers when he said, "As a mother, even at the risk of her own life, loves and protects her child, so let a man cultivate love without measure toward the whole world."

The Ancient Greeks celebrated Mother's Day in spring, like we do. They used to honor Rhea, "mother of the gods," with honey-cakes and fine drinks and flowers at dawn. Sounds like the beginnings of the Mother's Day tradition of breakfast in bed!

Mother's Day Delights Cookbook
A Collection of Mother's Day Recipes
Cookbook Delights Holiday Series-Book 5

Mother's Day History

Mother's Day History

Originally conceived by Julia Ward Howe after the American Civil War as a day honoring (in her opinion) the inherent pacifism of mothers, Mother's Day now simply celebrates motherhood. Mothers often receive gifts on this day.

Julia Ward Howe wrote the original Mother's Day Proclamation in 1870, as a call for peace and disarmament. Howe failed in her attempt to get formal recognition of a Mother's Day for Peace.

Her idea was influenced by Anna Jarvis, a young Appalachian homemaker who, starting in 1858, had attempted to improve sanitation through what she called Mothers' Work Days. She organized women throughout the Civil War to work for better sanitary conditions for both sides, and in 1868 she began work to reconcile Union and Confederate neighbors.

Jarvis' daughter, also named Anna Jarvis, would, of course, have known of her mother's work, and the work of Howe. Much later, when her mother died, this second Anna Jarvis started her own crusade to found a memorial day for women.

The first such Mother's Day was celebrated in Grafton, West Virginia, on May 10, 1908, in the church where the elder Anna Jarvis had taught Sunday School. Grafton is the home to the International Mother's Day Shrine. From there, the custom caught on — spreading eventually to 45 states. Finally the holiday was declared official by states beginning in 1912, and in 1914 the President, Woodrow Wilson, declared the first national Mother's Day.

Mother's Day Delights Cookbook
A Collection of Mother's Day Recipes
Cookbook Delights Holiday Series-Book 5

Mother's Day
Nutrition and Health

Mother's Day Nutrition and Health

Mother's Day is often celebrated with food: Either children cook for their mother, or, if children are very young, the husband makes a special meal for the mother of his children.

In *Mother's Day Delights Cookbook* we have included many nutritious recipes that incorporate the old-time staples of mom's home cooked meals as well as some of the new recipes that we hope you will make into new Mother's Day traditions.

If you are one of the many folks who entertain during this special day for honoring mother, the sections on appetizers and dips, beverages, and salads will be of great assistance by ensuring that your guests and families will be served nutritious and healthy foods for those quick get-togethers. If you are hosting dinners, the sections on main dishes, soups, side dishes, and others, will give recipes that are hearty, while at the same time nutritious. It is important to keep in mind the need to replenish the body with healthy and nutritious foods.

We have even included recipes that younger children can help prepare to make Mother's day a truly special occasion. This cookbook is designed so that children can cook with their father and give their mother the day off. It also gives children the chance to showcase their culinary abilities. *Mother's Day Delights Cookbook* is designed to make it easy for them to create a nutritious menu for a mother's special day.

However you celebrate this special day, be sure to have fun in your celebrations to create some cherished memories for everyone to enjoy.

Mother's Day Delights Cookbook
A Collection of Mother's Day Recipes
Cookbook Delights Holiday Series-Book 5

Poetry

A Collection of Poetry with Mother's Day Themes

Table of Contents

Page

Dear Daughter of Mine

Dear daughter of mine
With beautiful eyes a
Doorway to a kind soul,
A heart that trusts,
So much love to give.
You gave your love,
True and sincere,
To the love of your life;
You thought.
You planned to share long years
Together with your love.
Sadly, plans abruptly changed
As your "love"
Betrayed you.
Pain and tears fill your heart
And now you deeply grieve.
Misery as dark as death.
How I wish I could lift your anguish
And bring back your carefree smile.
Many times I think of you
And yearn to wash away your sorrow.
You are good and kind.
It is a mystery to us all
Why you have this burden
Inflicted only because you loved.
Loved with such a trusting heart.
I know not why this sincere heart
Betrayed you with such malice.
Please know that you are loved,
With all our hearts;
And these hearts will not betray
Your love or trust.
Also know that this will pass
Like gray clouds in the storm,
Drift away in darkness.
Once again the sun will shine

And sparkle on the flowers.
You will then wave goodbye
To dark and gloomy storms
That hung deep within your chest.
Stars will trip again the light fantastic
And twinkle in your heart.
Yes, your soul will glow again
And rejuvenate clear sky.

Karen Jean Matsko Hood ©2014
Published in *Mother's Day Delights Cookbook*, 2014
By Whispering Pine Press International, Inc., 2014

Moonlit Sun

How long will be my life?
I asked under the sunlit moon.
It seems I want to trade
My days of the magical
Worker bee with the giant
Sea turtle to bask in the
Hushful moonlit sun.

Karen Jean Matsko Hood ©2014
Published in *Mother's Day Delights Cookbook*, 2014
By Whispering Pine Press International, Inc., 2014

Carpenter's Daughter

Oak and pine and cedar bouquets,
perfumed sachet of wood.
Milky skin, fragrant parings
foreign to her nature.
Twilight calls this mind that sleeps
as hammer music talks outside.
Quiet follows saw blades breaking,
rusty on the earthen clay.
Splinters fly from the swaying sawhorse
trembling on the floor.
Nails pop through the pocket cloth
of the aging elder's apron.
Sawdust scents the room of the
sleeping carpenter's daughter.

Karen Jean Matsko Hood ©2014
Published in *Mother's Day Delights Cookbook*, 2014
By Whispering Pine Press International, Inc., 2014

Conception

My life began
at conception,
simple cells,
those sperm
and egg,
create
new life
unknown.

Mystery of
the ocean
bloom
swells warm
within the womb.

Soul
and
body
blend,
spirit deep,
wet darkness.

Energy of life
unknown
becomes
a shadow,
yet unborn.

Karen Jean Matsko Hood ©2014
Published in *Mother's Day Delights Cookbook*, 2014
By Whispering Pine Press International, Inc., 2014

I Love You

I love you more than beargrass,
    that blows in the wind.

I love you more than the fleabane,
    that undulates in the meadow.

I love you more than glacial streams
    that fall from clay cliffs.

I love you more than the blades of grass
    that wave in cool breezes.

I love you more than azure skies
    that drift across tall mountains.

My love grows far beyond the words
    written on the page.

My love for you is beauty beyond
perfection;
    joy completes my craving.

Karen Jean Matsko Hood ©2014
Published in *Mother's Day Delights Cookbook*, 2014
By Whispering Pine Press International, Inc., 2014

Motherly Gardening

My mother
Taught me
To garden
To dig with bare hands
In clay and
Loam,
And crawl with
Montana angleworms,
That shine in dim
Rays that reflect
From Big
Sky.

My mind
Wanders
Through the muck,
Reddish heavy,
Muddy ooze.
Intrigued with
Life
And worms,
Those bugs
Slink through
The gumbo,
Slip
in its
Heaviness.

Great Falls' wind
Reminds
Me to
Plant those
Seeds
Before Chinook
Winds come
To make
More mud.

Wise old mom
Knew that
Earthen mire
Grounded me
In ways
Earthworms
Inch and
Always understand.

Karen Jean Matsko Hood ©2014
Published in *Mother's Day Delights Cookbook*, 2014
By Whispering Pine Press International, Inc., 2014

Servant Woman

She walked barefoot
Holding a silver platter
Upon her head.

She walked proudly
And full of spirit, even
If her feet were fissured and weary.

This woman with ebony skin
And warm brown eyes
And proud posture.

Her hands and feet were
Aged, cracked
And wrinkled

Beyond her years.
We ordered off the menu
And she served us standing

At the table.
Scrumptious foods,
Wonderful spirits

Filled our table drinks
And then, lodged in my throat
Unable to swallow.

Haitian servant
Slave to tourists
Mother of nine.

Karen Jean Matsko Hood ©2014
Published in *Mother's Day Delights Cookbook*, 2014
By Whispering Pine Press International, Inc., 2014

Daylilies

Daylilies call out with
lax, savory whispers.
Fragile free forms: spritely lemon,
    ochre, chartreuse, and crimson,
waving in carefree meadows.
Seconds race by and ask their song.

Shy daylilies unfold and reveal the
  perfection of form enclosed within
numerous pods.
Each a foe of hours,
friend of minutes,
only one short day the Creator granted
    to chant a chorus of lullabies
with compelling reflection.
Fill the vase, not empty it.
Bouquets of colorful charm,
languish for attention
    in refractory,
deep cut crystal.

Karen Jean Matsko Hood ©2014
Published in *Mother's Day Delights Cookbook*, 2014
By Whispering Pine Press International, Inc., 2014

Lady's Slippers

Lady's slippers dance on tiptoes,
Blossoms unfold to mornings
Rosy glow. Shining vermilion illumines.
Chickadees scold the waking chipmunks.

Snapping turtles dig holes slowly,
While squirrels wrestle in the oak trees.
Lake mist rises above the stone wall,
As goldfish circle the lily pads.

Tamarack boughs edge toward the road,
Which winds through the cattails,
And beckons the mallards
To strut along the spring.

The display ends all too soon,
When evening shadows surrender
Sanguine skies, blocked by amber glow.
Midnight covers the celestial sphere,
       and all is still.

Karen Jean Matsko Hood ©2014
Published in *Mother's Day Delights Cookbook*, 2014
By Whispering Pine Press International, Inc., 2014

Mother's Day Delights Cookbook
A Collection of Mother's Day Recipes
Cookbook Delights Holiday Series-Book 5

Mother's Day Quotes

Mother's Day Quotes

A mother is a mother still, the holiest thing alive.
Samuel Taylor Coleridge

Youth fades; love droops, the leaves of friendship fall;
A mother's secret hope outlives them all.
Oliver Wendell Holmes, physician and poet

A mother understands what a child does not say.
Jewish Proverb

This heart, my own dear mother, bends,
With loves true instinct, back to thee!
Thomas Moore

I remember my mother's prayers and they have always
followed me. They have clung to me all my life.
Abraham Lincoln, U.S. President

A mother is the truest friend we have, when trials, heavy
and sudden, fall upon us; when adversity takes the place of
prosperity; when friends who rejoice with us in our
sunshine, desert us when troubles thicken around us, still
will she cling to us, and endeavor by her kind precepts and
counsels to dissipate the clouds of darkness, and cause
peace to return to our hearts.
Washington Irving 1783-1859

There never was a woman like her. She was gentle as a
dove and brave as a lioness. The memory of my mother
and her teachings were, after all, the only capital I had to
start life with, and on that capital I have made my way.
Andrew Jackson, U.S. President

There is no velvet as soft as a mother's lap, no rose as
lovely as her smile, no path as flowery as that imprinted
with her footsteps.
Archibald Thompson

Mother's Day Delights Cookbook
A Collection of Mother's Day Recipes
Cookbook Delights Holiday Series-Book 5

RECIPES

Mother's Day Delights Cookbook
A Collection of Mother's Day Recipes
Cookbook Delights Holiday Series-Book 5

Appetizers and Dips

Table of Contents

Page

Ahi Tuna Appetizer

Sashimi tuna marinade and this wasabi sauce is a favorite appetizer of my husband, my daughter Marissa, and mine. Use the freshest tuna you can find along with the best avocado and cucumber for a wonderful flavor.

Ingredients for appetizer:

¾ lb. sashimi grade tuna steak, diced
½ c. cucumber, diced
¼ c. green onion, chopped
1½ tsp. red pepper flakes
1 Tbs. sesame seeds, toasted
1½ tsp. lemon juice
2 tsp. sesame oil
½ c. soy sauce
1 avocado, peeled, pitted, diced
½ c. fresh tomatoes, diced
salt and pepper, to taste
romaine lettuce leaves, for garnish

Ingredients for wasabi sauce:

3 Tbs. wasabi powder
¼ c. mayonnaise
¼ c. sour cream
½ c. prepared Dijon style mustard
2 Tbs. hot pepper sauce
¼ c. green onion, chopped
salt and pepper, to taste

Directions for wasabi sauce:

1. In medium bowl, blend wasabi, mayonnaise, sour cream, mustard, and hot pepper sauce.
2. Mix in green onion; add salt and pepper, to taste.
3. Cover and refrigerate until ready to serve.

Directions for appetizer:

1. Heat a dry skillet over medium heat.
2. Add sesame seeds; cook 3 minutes until toasted and fragrant, stirring often to prevent burning; set aside.
3. In medium bowl, combine tuna, cucumber, green onion, red pepper flakes, and toasted sesame seeds.
4. Pour in lemon juice, sesame oil, and soy sauce; toss lightly.
5. Add avocado pieces; toss just enough to mix.
6. Place bowl into a large bowl filled with crushed ice.
7. Chill bowls in refrigerator for 15 minutes, but no longer, or the delicious freshness of the fish will be lost.
8. Once chilled, remove bowls from refrigerator and remove bowl from ice bowl, and invert on a lettuce-lined serving plate.
9. Sprinkle with tomatoes, and serve with toasted bread or your favorite crackers.
10. Serve wasabi sauce along side.

Coconut Dip

This is an easy-to-make dip that is especially good with fresh fruit.

Ingredients:

⅔ c. sour cream
⅓ c. coconut cream
⅓ c. brown sugar, firmly packed

Directions:

1. In small bowl, mix ingredients together.
2. Use as a dip for fruits such as orange sections, fresh pineapple spears, fresh figs, apricots, or banana slices.

Alaskan King Crab Cocktail

Our family loves crab, and this makes a delicious appetizer for special occasions.

Ingredients for crab cocktail:

> 1   c. Alaskan king crab meat
> 1½ c. red and yellow peppers, finely chopped
> ½   c. sweet onion, chopped
> 1½ c. celery, finely chopped
>   lettuce or spinach leaves, to line serving dish

Ingredients for cocktail sauce:

> 1   c. ketchup
> 2   Tbs. horseradish
> 2   tsp. hot sauce
> 1   tsp. white pepper
> 1   tsp. black pepper
> 1   tsp. salt
> ½   tsp. garlic powder
> 1   tsp. onion powder

Directions for cocktail:

1. Line a serving dish with lettuce or spinach leaves.
2. In large mixing bowl, combine crabmeat, red and yellow peppers, onion, and celery together.
3. Toss gently, so that the large lumps of crabmeat are not broken.
4. Heap crabmeat mixture on the greens.
5. Spoon cocktail sauce over the salad; chill.

Directions for cocktail sauce:

1. In medium mixing bowl, combine ketchup, horseradish, and hot sauce; blend well.

2. Season with both peppers, to taste.
3. Add salt, garlic, and onion powder; blend well.
4. Place in refrigerator; chill 1 hour.

Yields: 12 servings.

Fried Green Tomatoes

Our family loves fried green tomatoes. They are delicious served while hot.

Ingredients:

½ c. canola oil
4 lg. green tomatoes
2 c. flour
2 eggs, beaten
    salt and pepper, to taste
    Parmesan cheese (optional)

Directions:

1. In large skillet, over medium-high heat, add oil and heat.
2. Slice tomatoes ¼-inch thick and pat dry.
3. Place flour in a small bowl.
4. Dip tomatoes into beaten eggs; dredge them one at a time in the flour.
5. Place in oil and fry for 2 minutes.
6. Flip tomato and fry on the other side another 2 minutes.
7. Add additional oil as needed to fry all tomato slices.
8. Remove from skillet; sprinkle with salt and pepper to taste.
9. Serve while hot; sprinkle lightly with Parmesan cheese.

Antipasto

Antipasto makes a great appetizer that is colorful and light. Pack in decorative jars to give as gifts. Remember to select the freshest vegetables for the best results. Omit tuna for vegetarians.

Ingredients:

4   c. cauliflower, chopped
4   c. pearl onions
2   c. red bell peppers, chopped
2   c. yellow bell peppers, chopped
2   c. celery, chopped
2   cucumbers, peeled, seeded, chopped
2   c. carrots, chopped
2   c. olive oil
4   garlic cloves, peeled, sliced
2   c. distilled white vinegar
1   can tomato paste (6 oz.)
1   Tbs. pickling spice, wrapped in cheesecloth
1   c. pitted black olives, halved
1½ c. pitted green olives, halved
4   c. canned mushrooms, sliced
2   cans white albacore tuna, drained, flaked (6 oz. ea.)
    salt

Directions:

1. In large bowl, with enough lightly salted water to cover, place cauliflower, onions, both peppers, celery, and cucumbers together.
2. Soak 8 to 12 hours, or overnight.
3. In separate bowl, place carrots with enough lightly salted water to cover.
4. Soak 8 to 12 hours, or overnight.
5. In large saucepan, place olive oil, garlic, vinegar, tomato paste, and pickling spice.

6. Bring mixture to boil.
7. Drain and rinse carrots; add to tomato paste mixture.
8. Boil 10 minutes.
9. Drain and rinse vegetables.
10. Add to tomato paste and carrot mixture.
11. Cook entire mixture 10 more minutes, or until the cauliflower is tender, but crisp.
12. Stir olives, mushrooms, and tuna into the mixture.
13. Remove from heat.
14. Discard wrapped pickling spice.
15. While still hot, process following directions for canning on page 228.
16. May also be frozen in sterile, airtight containers, for up to 3 months.

Dip for Fresh Vegetables

This dip is flavorful and great to serve with your favorite vegetables.

Ingredients:

1 tsp. soy sauce
¼ c. sweet chili sauce
½ c. peanut butter, extra crunchy
¼ c. coconut milk powder
½ c. water, boiling

Directions:

1. In blender, add all ingredients.
2. Blend until smooth.
3. Refrigerate 2 hours.
4. Place dip in serving bowl on large platter.
5. Surround with cold, crisp vegetables.

Fried Wontons

These are very popular with all of my children. I double the recipe, and still, they disappear.

Ingredients for wontons:

- 1 pkg. wonton skins
- 1 egg white
  canola oil, for deep-frying

Ingredients for filling:

- 1 lb. ground pork
- 3 green onions, chopped
- ⅛ tsp. five spice powder
- 2 tsp. sesame oil
- 1 egg yolk
- 1 tsp. corn or potato starch
  dash of pepper

Ingredients for sauce:

- ½ c. ketchup
- 3 Tbs. brown sugar
- ¼ c. red wine or apple cider vinegar
- 1 tsp. cornstarch
- 1 tsp. cinnamon
  dash nutmeg and cloves

Directions for wontons and filling:

1. In large mixing bowl, add ground pork, green onions, and spice powder; mix well.
2. Add sesame oil, egg yolk, starch, and pepper to taste.
3. Lay out wonton skins.
4. Place 1 tablespoon filling in center of each skin.
5. Brush edge with egg white; fold diagonally to seal.
6. Preheat oil to 350 degrees F.

7. Deep-fry until light brown.
8. Drain on paper towels; place on serving plate.

Directions for sauce:

1. In small saucepan, mix together the ketchup, brown sugar, and wine or vinegar until blended.
2. Add cornstarch and spices; bring to boil.
3. Reduce heat; simmer 2 minutes.
4. Cool and serve with wontons.

Strawberry Cheese Ring

This is a delicious appetizer for any special occasion. Serve with a basket of assorted crackers, bagel chips, or bread sticks for dipping. If you need a smaller amount, reduce each ingredient by one-half.

Ingredients:

1 lb. sharp Cheddar cheese, grated
1 c. pecans, chopped
¾ c. mayonnaise
1 sm. onion, grated
1 med. garlic clove, minced
½ tsp. hot sauce
1 c. strawberry preserves

Directions:

1. Mix all ingredients, except preserves, together.
2. Lightly spray a 1-quart ring mold with cooking spray.
3. Press mixture into mold; chill thoroughly.
4. When ready to serve, unmold onto a serving plate.
5. Spoon preserves into center of ring; serve.
6. Place serving dish on a bed of crushed ice to extend length of time for use. Discard any unused cheese mixture after it has warmed to room temperature.

Egg Rolls

Egg rolls are always popular in our home. Our daughter Marissa took over making most of the egg rolls for the family, and we always enjoy it when she does. These egg rolls use a mixture of chicken, pork, and crab for a great flavor.

Ingredients:

2   lb. ground chicken
2   lb. ground pork
2   onions, chopped
1   bag bean sprouts
1   bag dry mushrooms
1½ tsp. pepper
3   tsp. salt
1   pkg. egg roll wrappers
3   eggs, separated
1   lb. frozen crab meat, finely chopped, or shredded
    canola oil, for frying

Directions:

1. In skillet, sauté chicken, pork, and onion for 5 minutes; place into a large bowl to cool.
2. In medium bowl, soak bean sprouts and mushrooms in warm water for 10 minutes; drain, chop, and add to meat mixture.
3. Mix in salt, pepper, and 3 egg yolks; add crab last.
4. Place spoonfuls on wrapper, seal edges with remaining egg whites, and roll.
5. In large skillet, heat oil to 350 degrees F.
6. Fry egg rolls; egg rolls are done when they turn brown.
7. Remove from oil.
8. Drain on paper towels.
9. Serve while warm.

Crispy Coconut Shrimp

This is an easy-to-make shrimp dish that can be served as a main dish or an appetizer.

Ingredients:

½ c. flour
1   Tbs. sugar
1   tsp. ground red pepper
½ tsp. salt
2   eggs
2   Tbs. water
2½ c. coconut, sweetened, flaked
1   lb. lg. shrimp, tails left on
2   c. canola oil

Directions:

1. In medium bowl, combine flour, sugar, red pepper, and salt.
2. In small bowl, beat together eggs and water.
3. Place coconut in shallow dish.
4. Coat shrimp with flour, dip in egg.
5. Roll in coconut, pressing firmly to coat both sides of shrimp.
6. Heat oil.
7. Cook shrimp in batches until golden brown.
8. Drain on a paper towel.
9. Note: A good dipping sauce is made with plain yogurt and pina colada mixer.

Did You Know? . . . .

Did you know that in the Bible, Eve is credited with being the "Mother of All the Living?"

Fried Calamari

Our family all enjoy these except for our two vegetarians. This simple recipe produces calamari that are, at once crispy, tender, and flavorful. As with all fried foods, they are best when served hot with your favorite cocktail or tartar sauce.

Ingredients:

> 1 lb. calamari, cleaned bodies and tentacles, or buy calamari rings already prepared
> 1 c. flour
> canola or peanut oil
> salt and pepper, to taste
> kosher salt

Directions:

1. Rinse calamari in a colander; place on a dinner plate.
2. Using scissors, cut calamari into 4 rings.
3. In Dutch oven, over medium-high heat, add 1 inch of oil.
4. Place a candy thermometer on the inside of the pot rim and heat oil until it reaches 375 degrees F.
5. In large bowl, place flour, salt and pepper to taste; blend well.
6. When oil is almost to temperature, add 5 rings and a few tentacles into the flour; stir with a fork, coating well.
7. Place floured rings in a fine mesh strainer.
8. Shake over flour bowl to shake off excess flour.
9. When oil is 375 degrees F., use a strainer to gently lower the calamari into the oil.
10. Stir, using the strainer, 2 minutes. When the calamari is browned, remove with the strainer to a paper towel-lined plate to drain.

11. Sprinkle with kosher salt and repeat with another batch of calamari.
12. Eat the fried calamari as it is cooked, or keep it warm in a 250 degree F. oven until ready to eat.
13. Serve with your favorite cocktail or tartar sauce.

Strawberry Cheese Ball

This cheese ball tastes great served with celery sticks or your favorite crackers, and it also makes a great gift to give to others.

Ingredients:

> 1 c. pecans, finely chopped
> ½ c. fresh parsley, chopped
> 1 c.. Colby cheese, grated
> 1 c. blue cheese, crumbled
> 1 pkg. cream cheese, softened (8 oz.)
> 1 tsp. fresh garlic, minced
> 1 Tbs. hot sauce
> 2 tsp. hot pepper sauce
> 1 c. strawberries, hulled, mashed

Directions:

1. Combine pecans and parsley in a small bowl, set aside; reserving 1 tablespoon.
2. In large bowl, combine cheeses, garlic, hot sauce, strawberries, and hot pepper sauce; mix until well blended.
3. Chill mixture in refrigerator for 1 hour.
4. Form chilled cheese mixture into ball shape.
5. Roll ball in pecan and parsley mixture.
6. Serve on center of a salad plate; garnish with reserved tablespoon of pecan and parsley mixture scattered around the ball on plate.

Spinach Artichoke Dip

This is a very tasty and easy-to-make spinach and artichoke dip.

Ingredients:

- ¼ c. olive oil
- 2 Tbs. butter
- ¾ c. white or yellow onion, finely chopped
- 1½ Tbs. garlic, minced
- ½ c. flour
- 1½ c. chicken stock, preferably homemade (use vegetable broth for vegetarians)
- 1½ c. heavy cream
- ¾ c. Parmesan cheese, freshly grated
- 2 Tbs. dehydrated chicken stock base or crumbled bouillon cubes (use vegetable broth for vegetarians)
- 1½ Tbs. lemon juice, freshly squeezed
- 1 tsp. sugar
- ¾ c. sour cream
- 1 pkg. frozen spinach, thawed, drained, wrung out (12 oz.)
- 1 can artichoke hearts, drained, sliced (6 oz.)
- 1 c. Monterey jack cheese, finely shredded
- ¾ tsp. red pepper sauce
  blue and white corn tortilla chips

Directions:

1. In large saucepan, over medium heat, warm olive oil and butter together.
2. When butter has melted, add onion and cook, stirring occasionally, 3 to 4 minutes, or until wilted.
3. Stir in garlic.
4. Cook 2 to 3 minutes longer, stirring frequently and stopping before the onion and garlic turn brown.

5. Sprinkle with flour and continue cooking, stirring continuously 10 to 15 minutes, or until mixture turns a golden blond color.
6. Whisking mixture continuously, slowly pour in the stock until it is smoothly incorporated.
7. When mixture begins to simmer, stir in cream.
8. Return to simmer.
9. Remove from heat.
10. Add Parmesan, chicken base or bouillon cubes, lemon juice, and sugar; stir until thoroughly blended.
11. Add sour cream, spinach, artichoke hearts, Monterey jack cheese, and red pepper sauce.
12. Stir until thoroughly combined and cheese has melted.
13. Transfer to a warmed serving bowl.
14. Serve immediately, accompanied by blue and white corn tortilla chips.

Peach Dip

This is an easy peach dip to make. Serve with your favorite fruits.

Ingredients:

    2   peaches, cut into chunks
    ½   c. sour cream or plain nonfat yogurt
    2   Tbs. brown sugar, packed
    1½ tsp. lemon juice

Directions:

1. In blender container, process all ingredients for 12 to 15 seconds, or until smooth.
2. Refrigerate for 1 hour before serving.

Strawberry Glazed Meatballs

This is a wonderful appetizer that is great for a buffet table.

Ingredients for meatballs:

1   lb. ground ham
1   lb. ground pork
2   eggs, well beaten
1   c. milk
2   c. bread crumbs
    salt and pepper, to taste

Ingredients for sauce:

1   c. brown sugar, firmly packed
½   c. strawberry preserves
1   Tbs. dry mustard
1¾ c. water
½   c. white vinegar

Directions for meatballs:

1. In large bowl, combine ham, pork, and eggs; blend well.
2. In medium bowl, combine milk, bread crumbs, and salt.
3. Stir into meat mixture; blend well.
4. Form into 1-inch meatballs and set aside.

Directions for sauce:

1. Preheat oven to 325 degrees F.
2. In small saucepan, combine sugar, mustard, and preserves; blend well.
3. Add vinegar and water to mixture; mix well.
4. Pour over meatballs.
5. Bake 1 hour, basting frequently.
6. Drain or skim off fat.
7. Serve in a chafing dish or crock-pot with toothpicks on the side.

Mother's Day Delights Cookbook
A Collection of Mother's Day Recipes
Cookbook Delights Holiday Series-Book 5

Beverages

Table of Contents

Page

Orange Frosty

Our kids always enjoy orange frosties. Try this easy to make recipe for your homemade orange frosties.

Ingredients:

6 oz. frozen orange juice concentrate
¼ c. sugar
1 c. milk
1 tsp. vanilla extract
1 c. water
8 ice cubes

Directions:

1. In blender container, combine orange juice, sugar, milk, vanilla, and water, blending well.
2. Add ice cubes one at a time; blend until smooth.
3. Pour into chilled glasses to serve.

Fresh Ginger Ale

When I was growing up, my mom gave me ginger ale whenever I did not feel well. I continue this tradition with my children. Some of them prefer ginger ale out of bottles, but I prefer this homemade version. Ginger is known to be a natural remedy to help soothe stomach ailments.

Ingredients:

2 lg. pieces fresh ginger, peeled, coarsely chopped
3½ strips lemon peel, white pith removed
4 c. water
1½ c. sugar
3 qt. club soda, chilled
   ice cubes

Directions:

1. In 4-quart saucepan, place ginger, lemon peel, and water.
2. Bring to boil; continue to boil for 10 minutes.
3. Stir in sugar; boil 15 minutes more.
4. Liquid should have been reduced to 3 cups.
5. Pour through a wire sieve and discard lemon peel and ginger.
6. Cool the syrup; cover, and chill 1 hour.
7. To serve, pour ¼ cup of syrup over ice cubes into a tall glass and add 1 cup of club soda.
8. Add more syrup to taste, if needed.

Yields: 12 servings.

Limeade

Limes are so refreshing. Try this delicious limeade with added limes and strawberries for flavor and bright color.

Ingredients:

6   c. water
2   c. fresh lime juice (12 limes)
1¼ c. sugar
    ice
    fresh lime slices, for garnish
    fresh strawberries, for garnish

Directions:

1. In large container, mix water and lime juice together; add sugar, stirring until sugar is dissolved.
2. Pour over ice in chilled glasses.
3. Garnish with fresh lime slices and strawberries.

Mango Lassi

We adopted our tenth child, our beautiful daughter, from India. These mango lassies are popular in Indian restaurants. Our family loves them. Enjoy!

Ingredients:

- 2 c. mango pulp, best quality
- 2 c. yogurt
- ½ c. sugar
- 1 c. crushed ice

Directions:

1. In blender, place mango pulp, yogurt, and sugar; blend until smooth.
2. Add crushed ice and blend again.
3. Pour into chilled glasses to serve.

Chocolate Malt Shake

Our family loves chocolate malts. Be sure to taste both the vanilla and chocolate malts to see which you enjoy more.

Ingredients:

- 1 pt. premium chocolate ice cream
- ¼ c. whole milk (more if you like a thinner milkshake)
- 1 Tbs. malt, add more to taste, if desired
- 2 Tbs. chocolate syrup

Directions:

1. In a blender, place all ingredients; process 30 to 45 seconds until well blended and smooth.
2. Pour into chilled glasses to serve.

Lemonade

Fresh squeezed lemons make a great drink. This homemade lemonade is refreshing and soothing to serve any time.

Ingredients:

    6 c. water
    2 c. lemon juice (8 lemons)
    1 c. sugar
        lemon or orange slices (optional)
        fresh mint leaves (optional)

Directions:

1. In large container, mix water, lemon juice, and sugar; stir until sugar is dissolved.
2. Pour over ice in chilled glasses.
3. Garnish with lemon slices and mint.

Blueberry Milkshake

This makes a delicious, easy-to-make blueberry milkshake. It is a great drink for those special occasions.

Ingredients

    1 c. vanilla ice cream
    1 c. whole milk or cream
    ¾ c. frozen blueberries
    1 tsp. vanilla extract
        honey, to taste

Directions:

1. In blender container, combine ice cream, milk, and vanilla; whirl until smooth.
2. Add honey to taste; blend well.
3. Add blueberries; whirl until berries are as fine as you like them.
4. Pour into chilled glasses and enjoy.

Brown Cow

When I was little, my cousins used to make brown cows and serve them when I would stay overnight. My children now enjoy them as an occasional treat.

Ingredients:

- 2 scoops vanilla ice cream
- 1 Tbs. chocolate syrup
- 10 oz. root beer
- 1½ oz. whipped cream
  - maraschino cherries

Directions:

1. In a large tumbler glass, combine ice cream and chocolate syrup.
2. Slowly pour root beer over the top.
3. Garnish with whipped cream and a cherry.
4. Serve with a straw and a long spoon.

Hot Cocoa

Nothing is more soothing on a cool day than hot cocoa. Serve with your choice of marshmallows, sweetened whipped cream, or cinnamon.

Ingredients:

- ½ c. unsweetened cocoa
- ½ c. sugar
- 3 c. hot water
- 2 tsp. vanilla extract
- 2 qt. milk
  - marshmallows, whipped cream, or cinnamon

Directions:

1. In medium saucepan, combine cocoa and sugar.
2. Gradually stir in water and vanilla to make a smooth paste.
3. Bring to boil; simmer 10 minutes.
4. In 3-quart saucepan, over low heat, scald milk.
5. Stir in cocoa mixture.
6. Cover; let stand over lowest heat, simmering for 30 minutes to mellow flavors.
7. Top with your choice of toppings and serve hot.

Yields: 12 cups.

Hot Apple Spiced Cider

Our family really enjoys the scent of warm aromatic spices as they heat over the stove. This would make a great hot drink to serve on Mother's Day.

Ingredients:

12 c. apple cider
1 tsp. whole cloves
½ tsp. ground nutmeg
4 sticks cinnamon

Directions:

1. In 3-quart saucepan, over medium-high heat, combine all ingredients.
2. Reduce heat; simmer uncovered, 10 minutes.
3. Strain cider mixture to remove cloves and cinnamon before serving.
4. Pour into large warmed mugs and serve hot.

Yields: 10 to 12 servings.

Peach Melba

This is a very tasty drink with combinations of peaches, cream, and berries.

Ingredients:

   16 oz. peach nectar
   4 scoops vanilla ice cream
   1 peach, pitted, peeled, chopped
   6 oz. berries of choice
      raspberries, for garnish

Directions:

   1. In blender container, combine nectar, ice cream, peach, and berries.
   2. Blend on low speed, until creamy and smooth, increasing speed if needed.
   3. Pour into chilled highball glasses and garnish with a sprinkling of raspberries.

Yields: 2 to 3 servings.

Hot Vanilla

This drink is such a refreshing change of pace to hot chocolate. By using fresh vanilla beans, it makes the fragrance and flavor absolutely enticing.

Ingredients:

   2 c. milk
   ¼ c. whipping cream
   1 vanilla bean
   1½ tsp. sugar
      ground cinnamon
      sweetened whipped cream, for garnish

Directions:

1. In heavy saucepan, over low heat, combine milk, whipping cream, vanilla bean, and sugar.
2. When small bubbles appear around the sides of the pan, remove from heat; let stand 15 to 20 minutes.
3. Place the pan back on the stove and warm mixture again, whisking briefly to redistribute the skin that forms on the milks surface.
4. Remove vanilla bean, carefully scrape out seeds with a sharp knife; return seeds to warmed milk.
5. Pour vanilla milk into two large mugs and top with sprinklings of cinnamon or vanilla bean, adding some whipped cream for extra taste.

Root Beer Floats

Our family loves root beer floats for a special treat. As a family, we make them every spring and summer for everyone to enjoy. A layer of whipped cream and maraschino cherries add a special touch.

Ingredients:

1 qt. vanilla ice cream
24 oz. root beer
1 c. whipped cream (optional)
8 maraschino cherries (optional)

Directions:

1. In four tall, chilled glasses, place 1 scoop of ice cream.
2. Pour root beer carefully over ice cream.
3. Add another scoop of ice cream and repeat with root beer.
4. If possible, repeat again; top with whipped cream and maraschino cherries.

Strawberry Frosty

This strawberry drink can be made year round if you have fresh, frozen strawberries stashed in the freezer.

Ingredients:

1¼ c. frozen strawberries
1   c. water
1   c. milk
2   Tbs. sugar
1   tsp. vanilla extract
    ice cubes (10-12)

Directions:

1. In blender container, combine strawberries, water, and milk; whirl briefly to blend.
2. Add sugar and vanilla.
3. Cover and blend, adding ice cubes one at a time; blend 30 seconds, or until smooth.
4. Serve immediately in chilled glasses.

Yields: 4 to 6 servings.

Chai Tea

This is a soothing drink for afternoon tea. Surprise your mom today with hot chai tea and some warm cookies fresh from the oven.

Ingredients:

4 c. water
8 bags black tea (8 tsp. loose)
4 c. milk
4 Tbs. honey, or to taste
1 tsp. ground ginger

1 tsp. ground nutmeg
½ tsp. ground cinnamon

Directions:

1. In 4-quart saucepan, heat water to boiling.
2. Add tea bags or loose tea in a strainer; reduce heat.
3. Simmer uncovered, 2 minutes.
4. Remove tea bags or strainer.
5. Add milk and honey; whisk to foam the milk.
6. Stir in ginger, nutmeg, and cinnamon to taste; heat to boiling point without boiling.
7. Whisk again; pour into heated cups and serve.

Yields: 8 servings.

Vanilla Malt Shake

Our family loves old-fashioned malts, and this recipe makes a full-flavored and delicious vanilla malt.

Ingredients:

1 c. cold milk
½ c. carbonated water
7 Tbs. malted milk powder, to taste
2 tsp. vanilla extract
4 scoops premium vanilla bean ice cream

Directions:

1. In blender container, combine milk, carbonated water, malted milk powder, and vanilla extract.
2. Add ice cream.
3. Cover and blend until smooth.
4. Pour into chilled glasses to serve.

Yields: 2 servings.

Vanilla Milkshake

There is nothing like the great taste of a frosty cold vanilla milkshake.

Ingredients:

    2 scoops vanilla bean ice cream
    2 c. half and half cream
    2 tsp. vanilla extract

Directions:

1. In blender container, combine ice cream, half and half, and vanilla; blend until smooth.
2. Pour into chilled glasses and serve.
3. Note: Soften ice cream first for easier blending.
4. Thinner milkshakes, add more half and half.
5. Thicker milkshakes, add more ice cream.

Virgin Mary

Try serving this on Mother's day with your mom's breakfast to show her how much you value her health.

Ingredients:

    4 oz. tomato juice
    3 dashes lemon juice
    1 pinch celery salt
    6 drops hot sauce
    1 pinch coarse peppers
    3 drops hot sauce
    1 celery stalk
    couple of ice cubes

Directions:

1. In a large highball glass, pour tomato juice slowly over ice cubes.
2. Season to taste with additional ingredients, stir well.
3. Garnish with celery stalk.

Mother's Day Delights Cookbook
A Collection of Mother's Day Recipes
Cookbook Delights Holiday Series-Book 5

Breads and Rolls

Table of Contents

Page

Pizza Dough

Our family loves pizza, and Friday night dinner is family pizza night. We have fun in trying different recipes and toppings, always searching for the perfect pizza.

Ingredients:

    3 c. flour (not self rising)
    1 Tbs. sugar
    1 tsp. salt
    1 pkg. regular or quick active dry yeast
    3 Tbs. olive oil
    1 c. very warm water

Directions:

1. In large mixing bowl, mix 1 cup of flour, sugar, salt, and yeast.
2. Add 3 tablespoons oil and water.
3. With electric mixer on medium speed, beat 3 minutes, scraping bowl frequently.
4. Stir in enough of the remaining flour until dough is soft and leaves sides of bowl.
5. Place dough on lightly floured surface.
6. Knead 5 to 8 minutes, or until dough is smooth and elastic.
7. Cover loosely with plastic wrap; let rest 30 minutes.
8. Continue as directed below for thin or thick crusts.

For thin crusts:

1. Preheat oven to 425 degrees F.
2. Lightly grease two baking sheets or 12-inch pizza pans.
3. Divide dough in half.
4. Pat each half into 12-inch circle on baking sheets.
5. Partially bake, 7 to 8 minutes, or until crust just begins to brown.
6. Remove from oven; add toppings.
7. Bake another 7 to 8 minutes.
8. Cut into sections to serve.

For thick crusts:

1. Preheat oven to 375 degrees F.
2. Move rack to lowest position.
3. Lightly grease two 8 x 8 x 2-inch square baking pans, or two 9-inch round baking pans.
4. Sprinkle with cornmeal.
5. Divide dough in half; pat each half into bottom of pan.
6. Cover loosely with plastic wrap; let rise in warm place until almost double in bulk.
7. Bake 20 to 22 minutes, or until crust just begins to brown; remove from oven.
8. Add toppings; bake another 20 to 22 minutes.
9. Cut into sections to serve.

Coconut English Muffin Bread

This is an easy recipe to make in your bread machine. Enjoy!

Ingredients:

1¼ c. water
3   c. bread flour
2   tsp. sugar
3   Tbs. nonfat dry milk
1   tsp. salt
2   tsp. yeast
¼   tsp. baking soda
1   c. coconut

Directions:

1. Put all ingredients in machine in order suggested by your bread machines manufacturer, using regular bread cycle.
2. Note: This recipe makes a large loaf (1½ lb.); adjust ingredients for a medium or small size loaf.
3. Top of loaf should come out sunken; this is normal.

Basic Roll Recipe

This recipe can be used in so many ways that it is good to double the recipe while you are at it. The caramel rolls are delicious!

Ingredients:

 1½ c. milk
 2 pkg. yeast
 ½ c. lukewarm water
 2 tsp. salt
 ½ c. sugar
 2 eggs, beaten
 ½ c. shortening
 7-8 c. flour

Directions:

1. In medium saucepan, over medium heat, scald milk; cool.
2. Dissolve yeast in lukewarm water.
3. Add salt, sugar, and eggs to cool milk; mix well.
4. Add 2 cups of flour and mix well.
5. Add shortening, then enough of the remaining flour to make a stiff dough.
6. Turn onto a floured surface and knead until smooth.
7. Place in a greased bowl, cover, and let rise until double in bulk, 1½ hours.
8. Form into parker house, crescent, cloverleaf, or dinner rolls and place into greased pan.
9. Let rise until double.
10. Bake in a preheated oven at 375 degrees F. for 12 to 15 minutes.
11. Note: For hamburger buns, form the dough into large buns, 3 inches in diameter, and place them 2 inches apart on a greased baking sheet.
12. For Coney buns, shape into oblongs.

Variations:

Directions for cinnamon rolls:

1. After dough has risen once (number 7 on previous page), divide into two portions and roll out each half on a floured surface.
2. Spread with soft butter and sprinkle with sugar and cinnamon; add raisins, if desired.
3. Roll up and cut into 1-inch slices.
4. Place, cut side down, on a greased baking sheet or into an oblong pan.
5. Let rise until double in bulk; bake as stated in number 10 on previous page.
6. Remove from oven, place on wire rack to partially cool, frost with powdered sugar, frosting, or glaze.

Directions for caramel rolls:

1. In medium bowl, combine 1 cup brown sugar, 2 tablespoons corn syrup, 3 to 4 tablespoons water, ½ cup walnuts or pecans, and several small pieces of butter to form a syrup; spread into the bottom of an oblong pan.
2. Place the rolls, cut side down, in syrup mixture.
3. Continue as for cinnamon rolls.
4. When rolls are done baking, turn out of pan immediately, scraping the syrup from bottom over the rolls.

Directions for doughnuts:

1. After dough has risen once (number 7 on previous page), punch it down and roll it out on a floured surface to ½-inch thick.
2. Cut with a doughnut cutter.
3. Let rise about halfway, 20 to 30 minutes, and then fry in preheated oil at 400 degrees F., turning once, until medium brown on both sides.

79

4. Remove and drain on paper towels.
5. Cool to lukewarm.
6. Roll doughnuts in sugar.

Ingredients for maple bars:

1. Roll out dough as for doughnuts above.
2. Cut in oblongs 1½-inch wide x 4½-inches long.
3. Proceed frying the same as for doughnuts.
4. Remove from oil and drain on paper towels.
5. Cool.
6. Frost with maple-flavored powdered sugar frosting.

Whole Wheat Pizza Dough

Our family enjoys Friday night pizza. Some of us like the whole grain taste, while others prefer the white. To find out what you like, be sure and try them both.

Ingredients:

1 c. warm water (very warm, not hot)
1 pkg. yeast
1 Tbs. olive oil
1 tsp. salt
1 tsp. honey or sugar
2 c. whole wheat flour
   additional olive oil

Directions:

1. In large mixing bowl, mix together water, yeast, oil, salt, and honey; let stand 5 minutes or longer.
2. Add flour, mix well; place on floured surface, and knead at least 10 times.
3. Divide in half; let rest 5 minutes.
4. Press into two pizza pans oiled with olive oil.
5. Note: Lightly oil fingers to spread dough on pan.

Cherry Banana Bread

Maraschino cherries, banana, and macadamia nuts are a perfect trio in this quick bread.

Ingredients:

- 1 jar maraschino cherries (10 oz.)
- ⅓ c. butter, room temperature
- ⅔ c. brown sugar, firmly packed
- 2 eggs
- 1¾ c. flour
- 2 tsp. baking powder
- ½ tsp. salt
- 1 c. ripe bananas, mashed
- ½ c. macadamia nuts or walnuts, chopped

Directions:

1. Preheat oven to 350 degrees F.
2. Lightly grease a 9 x 5 x 3-inch loaf pan with cooking spray.
3. Drain cherries, reserving 2 tablespoons juice.
4. Coarsely chop cherries; set aside.
5. In large mixing bowl, combine butter, brown sugar, eggs, and reserved cherry juice.
6. With electric mixer on medium speed, beat 3 to 4 minutes until well mixed.
7. In medium bowl, sift together flour, baking powder, and salt; add to butter mixture alternately with mashed banana, beginning and ending with flour mixture.
8. Fold in cherries and nuts.
9. Spread batter evenly in pan.
10. Bake 1 hour, until golden brown, or until inserted toothpick in center comes out clean.
11. Remove from oven; turn out of pan onto wire rack.
12. Cool completely before slicing to serve.
13. Wrap in plastic wrap or store in airtight container for up to week.
14. This bread also freezes well.

Buttermilk Cloverleaf Rolls

These light and delicious rolls are always one of the favorites to serve for your special holiday dinners.

Ingredients:

½ c. butter
2 c. buttermilk
2 pkg. dry yeast
½ tsp. baking soda
2 Tbs. sugar
2 tsp. salt
5 c. flour
1 egg, slightly beaten
   additional butter

Directions:

1. In small saucepan, heat butter and buttermilk until very warm.
2. Combine with yeast and let stand 2 to 3 minutes until the yeast has dissolved.
3. Stir in baking soda, sugar, and salt.
4. Gradually stir in flour until the dough starts to leave the sides of the bowl.
5. Turn out and knead the dough on a floured work surface, adding more flour if sticky, until smooth and elastic, about 10 minutes.
6. Shape dough into a ball, put in a buttered bowl, and turn so that it is buttered all over.
7. Cover and let rise in warm place until double in bulk, about 45 minutes.
8. Butter three 6-cup muffin tins.
9. Punch dough down.
10. Divide into 18 portions; then form each portion into 3 balls.
11. Put 3 balls into each muffin cup.

12. Cover and let rise until double in size, about 30 minutes.
13. Brush tops of rolls with beaten egg.
14. Bake in a preheated oven at 400 degrees F. until the rolls are browned, 15 to 20 minutes.

Blueberry Muffins

Fresh blueberry muffins are delicious. These are best served right out of the oven with butter.

Ingredients:

1¾ c. flour
2   Tbs. sugar
2½ tsp. baking powder
¾   tsp. salt
1   egg, well beaten
¾   c. milk
¼   c. sugar
⅓   c. canola oil
½   c. fresh or frozen blueberries, drained

Directions:

1. Preheat oven to 400 degrees F.
2. Line muffin pans with paper cups.
3. In large bowl, sift together flour, sugar, baking powder, and salt.
4. Make a well in the center.
5. In separate bowl, combine egg, milk, sugar, and oil; add all at once to dry ingredients.
6. Stir quickly, until dry ingredients are just moistened.
7. Gently fold in blueberries.
8. Fill prepared pans ⅔ full.
9. Bake 25 minutes.
10. Turn out onto wire rack to cool.

Cornbread

This is a very tasty corn bread that is always good served hot out of the pan, and it's even tastier with butter and honey.

Ingredients:

 1 pkg. active dry or cake yeast
 ¼ c. water, very warm
 2 c. milk, scalded
 ⅓ c. sugar
 1 c. butter
 1 Tbs. salt
 7 c. flour, sifted
 2 eggs, well beaten
 1 c. yellow cornmeal

Directions:

1. Preheat oven to 350 degrees F.
2. Lightly grease a 9 x 13-inch baking pan.
3. In a measuring cup, sprinkle yeast into very warm water, stirring until dissolved.
1. In large mixing bowl, combine milk, sugar, butter, and salt.
2. Stir in 3 cups of the flour, blending well.
3. Stir in eggs, yeast mixture, and cornmeal until well blended.
4. Gradually add and stir in the remaining flour.
5. Spoon into prepared pan.
6. Place in warm area and let rise slightly.
7. Bake 25 to 30 minutes, or until inserted toothpick comes out clean.
8. Remove from oven.
9. Cool slightly and cut into squares.
10. Serve warm with butter.

Chocolate Date Muffins

These are very moist muffins with a wonderful texture. The combination of chocolate and dates is unusual but makes a very delicious muffin for breakfast or brunch.

Ingredients:

¾ c. seedless dates, finely chopped
¾ c. boiling water
½ c. butter, softened slightly
½ c. sugar
2 Tbs. walnuts or pecans, chopped
1 egg
1 tsp. vanilla extract
¼ tsp. baking soda
¼ c. milk
1¾ c. flour
½ c. chocolate, or chocolate chips, chopped

Directions:

1. Preheat oven to 350 degrees F.
2. Paper-line muffin pans or lightly spray with oil.
3. In large bowl, place dates; pour boiling water over them.
4. Add butter, in small pieces; stir until butter melts.
5. Add sugar; cool slightly.
6. Add walnuts, egg, and vanilla.
7. In measuring cup, mix baking soda with milk; add to butter mixture.
8. Add flour; stir just until combined.
9. Fold in chocolate; spoon into prepared muffin tins, filling just under ⅔ full.
10. Bake 20 minutes.
11. Remove from oven; turn out of pan.
12. Serve warm while chocolate is still runny.
13. Reheat any leftover muffins in a microwave oven.

English Crumpets

I love tea and always enjoy having it with the family. I used to read about tea and crumpets, and my daughters were the first to make me crumpets for a gift for my Mother's Day tea. It makes a nice tradition, and this is a recipe my entire family likes. They are delicious served warm with butter and fresh strawberry jam or homemade strawberry preserves.

Ingredients:

    1 c. flour
    1 c. bread flour
    4 tsp. salt
    1 Tbs. fresh yeast
    2 tsp. sugar
    2 c. warm milk
    2 Tbs. canola oil
    1 tsp. baking soda
    ½ c. warm water

Directions:

1. In large, warm bowl, sift flours and salt.
2. In small bowl, cream yeast and sugar; add warm milk and oil.
3. Stir into flour to make a batter; beat vigorously until smooth and elastic.
4. Cover bowl, put in a warm place; let stand 1½ hours until mixture rises and surface is full of bubbles.
5. Punch dough down by beating with wooden spoon.
6. Add baking soda mixed with ½ cup of warm water.
7. Cover; return to warm place for 30 minutes.
8. Heat bake stone or heavy skillet; lightly grease.
9. Grease six crumpet rings (3 to 3½-inch), or scone cutters, and put them on the stone or skillet to heat.
10. Cook as many as you can at a time, as batter will not stay bubbly for long.
11. Pour batter into each ring, ½-inch deep.
12. Cook gently 7 to 10 minutes, or until surface sets and is full of tiny bubbles.

13. Using an oven glove, lift off ring; if base of crumpet is pale gold, flip it over and cook 3 minutes until other side is the same.
14. If crumpet batter is set but sticks slightly in the ring, push it out gently with the back of a wooden spoon.
15. Wipe, grease, and heat rings for each batch of crumpets.
16. If serving immediately, wrap crumpets in a cloth and keep warm between batches.
17. Butter generously and serve at once.
18. Note: If reheating, toast crumpets under the grill, cooking smooth surface first and then the top so that the butter will melt into the holes.

Dumplings

These are another family favorite. They are great served as chicken and dumplings or on top of beef stew.

Ingredients:

3   c. flour
2   Tbs. parsley flakes (optional)
4   tsp. baking powder
1   tsp. salt
6   Tbs. butter
1½ c. milk

Directions:

1. In medium bowl, combine flour, parsley, baking powder, and salt.
2. Cut in butter until mixture looks like fine crumbs.
3. Stir in milk to make thick batter.
4. Drop dough by large spoonfuls onto hot meat or vegetables in boiling stew. Do not drop directly onto liquid or dumplings may become soggy.
5. Cook, uncovered, 10 minutes.
6. Cover; cook 10 minutes longer.
7. For herb dumplings, substitute 2 teaspoons chopped fresh basil, sage, thyme, or celery seed for the parsley.

Golden Pretzel

This is another great recipe that your whole family will delight in eating and will also want you to make often.

Ingredients:

    1 basic Danish pastry recipe (see recipe on page 90)
    1 egg
    ¼ c. almonds, toasted, coarsely ground
    ½ c. dried prunes, pitted
    ½ c. water
    ¼ c. sugar

Directions:

1. In small saucepan, combine prunes and water.
2. Simmer 30 minutes, or until prunes are very tender.
3. When cooled to warm, place in blender, stir in sugar and blend until smooth.
4. Set aside to cool completely.
5. Divide dough into quarters; chill or freeze three quarters of it to make more pretzels, if you wish.
6. Divide remaining quarter in half.
7. Roll out each to a long strip, 30 x 3-inches, on a lightly floured pastry cloth or parchment paper.
8. Spoon ¼ cup prune filling down the middle of each, then dampen edges and fold over filling to cover completely; overlap other edge over top ¼-inch (edges will open some during baking).
9. Lift carefully onto greased baking sheet; shape into a pretzel.
10. Cover; let rise in a warm place, away from draft, 1 hour, or until double in bulk.
11. Preheat oven to 450 degrees F.
12. Brush tops with slightly beaten egg; sprinkle generously with sugar, then sprinkle with almonds.
13. Place in oven; reduce heat to 375 degrees F.
14. Bake 20 minutes, or until golden brown.

Yields: 2 pretzels.

Irish Soda Bread

Try this old-fashioned soda bread still hot from the oven with lots of butter and jam, or honey for a real treat.

Ingredients:

8	c. flour
½	c. sugar
2	tsp. salt
2	tsp. baking powder
2	tsp. baking soda
½	c. butter
8	Tbs. caraway seed
4	c. raisins
2⅔	c. buttermilk
4	egg whites, beaten
	milk

Directions:

1. Preheat oven to 375 degrees F.
2. Lightly spray with cooking oil, two 7 x 4-inch loaf pans.
3. In large bowl, combine flour, sugar, salt, baking powder, and baking soda.
4. Cut in butter until mixture becomes a coarse meal.
5. Stir in caraway seeds and raisins.
6. In another bowl, combine buttermilk and egg.
7. Stir into dry mixture until moistened.
8. Turn out onto floured surface.
9. Knead lightly until smooth.
10. Shape dough into 2 balls.
11. Place into prepared pans.
12. Brush tops with milk.
13. Bake 1 hour, or until golden brown.
14. Turn out onto wire rack.
15. Serve hot out of the oven or cool.

Danish Pastry

Danish pastry is an excellent choice for basic dough when you want to try different kinds of fillings. By leaving the sugars out, the pastry may also be made into coverings for meats or veggies.

Ingredients for pastry:

¼ c. warm water
2 pkg. active dry yeast
1 c. milk
2 eggs, 1 of which has been slightly beaten
1 Tbs. sugar
3½ c. flour, sifted
1½ c. cold butter, sliced

Directions:

1. In large bowl, sprinkle yeast into ¼ cup warm water; let stand 3 to 5 minutes; stir.
2. Blend in milk, unbeaten egg, and half the flour; beat with wooden spoon until smooth.
3. Gradually stir in enough flour to make soft dough.
4. Turn out onto floured surface; let rest 30 minutes.
5. Gently roll dough to a 14 x 10-inch rectangle.
6. Cover ⅔ of rectangle with slices of butter, leaving 1-inch edge all around uncovered.
7. Sprinkle with 2 tablespoons flour.
8. Fold uncovered ⅓ of dough over buttered part and press edges together.
9. Gently roll in 14 x 10-inch rectangle, having long side parallel with front edge of surface.
10. Fold again from left and right, making 3 layers of dough; turn ¼ turn to the right.
11. Repeat rolling, folding, and turning 3 or 4 times, keeping to same size. If dough becomes sticky, wrap in wax paper; chill 15 minutes.
12. Roll into 18 x 15-inch rectangle, rubbing flour on surface and rolling pin, as needed.
13. Cut into 3-inch squares.

14. Put desired filling in centers of squares and fold corners to center, pinching points together.
15. Put on baking sheets; let rise at room temperature until almost double in bulk.
16. Preheat oven to 425 degrees F.
17. Beat remaining egg; brush tops of pastries carefully.
18. Bake 10 to 12 minutes.
19. Remove from oven and place on rack to cool.
20. If pastries are sweet, drizzle with powdered sugar glaze if desired.

Banana Nut Bread

This is a very tasty and moist bread. Our children love it warm right out of the oven and cold in their lunch. We double the recipe for our family.

Ingredients:

½   c. butter
1   c. sugar
2   eggs
3   bananas, overripe, mashed
¼   c. sour cream
1   tsp. baking soda
1   tsp. baking powder
1½ c. nuts, coarsely chopped
2½ c. flour, sifted

Directions:

1. Preheat oven to 350 degrees F.
2. Lightly grease a loaf pan.
3. In large mixing bowl, cream butter, sugar, and sour cream. Add eggs, one at a time, and beat well.
4. Add mashed bananas; mix well.
5. In another bowl, sift dry ingredients together; add nuts.
6. Add dry ingredients to cream mixture; mix well.
7. Pour into prepared pan.
8. Bake 50 minutes.

Mom's Whole Wheat Bread

For the first year we were married I made all our bread homemade. As the years have gone by, I have found homemade bread is still the greatest! Try this whole wheat version.

Ingredients:

¼ c. honey
2 Tbs. yeast
1 c. warm water
1 c. water
¾ c. canola oil
1 tsp. salt
¼ c. molasses
2 eggs, beaten
6 c. whole wheat bread flour

Directions:

1. In small bowl, combine honey, yeast, and warm water; let stand for 5 minutes.
2. In another small bowl, mix together 1 cup of water, oil, salt, molasses, and eggs, beating well.
3. Add this mixture to yeast mixture, blending well.
4. Add 3 cups of the flour; mix or beat, 5 minutes.
5. Continue adding 1 cup of flour at a time, just until dough is easy to handle.
6. Turn out onto floured surface and knead until dough is smooth and elastic. Be careful with flour additions, as too much flour will cause bread to be dry and crumbly.
7. Cover and let rise until double in bulk.
8. Punch bread down and form into loaves, placing in 2 or 3 lightly greased bread pans.
9. Cover; let rise in warm place, until double in bulk.
10. Preheat oven to 350 degrees F.

11. Bake 25 minutes, or until hollow sound when tapped on top.
12. Remove from oven; turn out onto wire rack to cool before slicing.
13. Note: This dough may also be used for cinnamon rolls or buns.

Popovers

I remember the first time I made popovers, when I was a teenager. Try these popovers served hot right out of the oven. They can be baked ahead and reheated. When it's time to eat, just reheat on an ungreased baking sheet at 350 degrees F. for 5 minutes.

Ingredients:

8 lg. eggs
4 c. flour
4 c. milk
2 tsp. salt

Directions:

1. Preheat oven to 450 degrees F.
2. Generously grease two 12-cup popover pans or twelve 12-ounce custard cups.
3. If using custard cups, place on baking sheet to bake.
4. In medium bowl, beat eggs slightly with fork or whisk.
5. Beat in remaining ingredients, just until smooth. Do not over beat, or popovers may not puff as high.
6. Fill cups half full.
7. Bake 20 minutes.
8. Reduce oven temperature to 325 degrees F. for popover pan, or 350 degrees F. for custard cup.
9. Bake 20 minutes longer, or until deep golden brown.
10. Immediately remove from cup and pierce each with sharp knife to let steam escape.
11. Serve while hot.

Oatmeal Rolls

These oatmeal rolls are great. I like them hot with butter or jam.

Ingredients:

1 pkg. active dry yeast
1 c. water, lukewarm
1 c. milk
¼ c. butter
3 Tbs. sugar
1 Tbs. salt
1 c. oatmeal, cooked
7 c. flour

Directions:

1. In small saucepan, cook oatmeal according to package directions to make 1 cup cooked oatmeal.
2. In small bowl, soften yeast in lukewarm water.
3. In small saucepan, scald milk, cool to lukewarm.
4. In large bowl, combine yeast mixture and milk.
5. Add butter, sugar, and salt; mix well.
6. Stir in cooked oatmeal.
7. Add flour, mixing until dough is stiff enough to handle.
8. Turn out onto a floured surface; knead until smooth.
9. Place in greased bowl and let rise until double in bulk; punch down and let rise once more.
10. Form into ping pong size-balls.
11. Place in greased muffin tins; let rise.
12. Bake in preheated oven at 400 degrees F., 12 minutes.
13. Turn out onto wire rack to cool.
14. Cool if desired, or serve hot out of the oven.

Yields: 3 to 4 dozen rolls.

Mother's Day Delights Cookbook
A Collection of Mother's Day Recipes
Cookbook Delights Holiday Series-Book 5

Breakfasts

Table of Contents

Page

Butterhorns

My mom and dad always used to buy butterhorns at the local bakery in Montana. They would heat them with butter and serve them with hot coffee or milk for a quick breakfast treat. I cannot find them in the bakery where I live, but this is a delicious recipe that is just as good. This recipe also makes a delicious Danish pastry.

Ingredients for butterhorns:

    2 pkg. yeast
    ¾ c. lukewarm water
    1 Tbs. sugar
    1 c. flour
    ½ c. butter, room temperature
    ¼ c. sugar
    1 tsp. salt
    6 egg yolks, beaten
    3 c. flour
       butter, softened
       powdered sugar glaze
       chopped nuts

Directions for butterhorns:

1. In small bowl, dissolve yeast and sugar in lukewarm water.
2. Blend in 1 cup of flour.
3. Cover and let rise until bubbly.
4. Cream butter with ¼ cup sugar until smooth.
5. In large bowl, mix together salt and egg yolks; add yeast mixture, stir.
6. Beat in remainder of flour, mix well.
7. Turn out onto floured surface and knead until smooth.
8. Place in greased bowl, turn dough to coat.
9. Cover and let rise until double.

10. Divide dough in half.
11. Roll each piece to a 6 x 18-inch rectangle on a lightly floured surface.
12. Spread center with soft butter.
13. Fold left half over center and spread with butter.
14. Fold right half over and spread with butter.
15. Roll out again and repeat procedure.
16. Roll out a third time and cut into 1-inch strips.
17. Coil each strip, snail fashion, on a greased baking sheet, leaving plenty of room between rolls.
18. Let rise until double.
19. Preheat oven to 375 degrees F.
20. Bake 12 to 15 minutes.
21. Remove from oven.
22. Place on a wire rack to cool.
23. Frost with powdered sugar frosting and sprinkle with chopped walnuts.

Directions for Danish pastry:

1. Follow same recipe and procedure as for butterhorns.
2. When rolled out the third time, cut in 4-inch squares.
3. Place tablespoonful of strawberry jam in center of each square.
4. Bring opposite corners together and pinch.
5. Place on greased baking sheet and let rise until double.
6. In small bowl, add beaten egg.
7. Brush on pastries with pastry brush; sprinkle with chopped nuts.
8. Preheat oven to 375 degrees F.
9. Bake 12 to 15 minutes.
10. Remove from oven.
11. Place on a wire rack.
12. While still warm, drizzle a thin powdered sugar glaze over the pastries.

Apple Fritters

This recipe was given to me by my mother and has been passed on through generations. These are great rolled in powdered sugar or cinnamon and sugar. I remember eating them for a special breakfast treat as a child and years later, I enjoy serving them to my family as a special treat during apple season.

Ingredients:

> 3 apples, finely chopped (select your favorite type)
> 2 eggs, well beaten
> 2 Tbs. canola oil
> ½ c. sugar
> 2 c. flour
> 2 tsp. baking powder
> 1 c. milk
>   canola oil, for frying
>   powdered sugar
>   sugar
>   cinnamon

Directions:

1. In large bowl, sift together flour, baking powder, and sugar.
2. In small bowl, beat together oil and eggs.
3. Add milk; mix well.
4. Blend liquid into flour mixture, mixing thoroughly.
5. Add apples and stir until combined.
6. In large skillet, heat oil to 400 degrees F.
7. Drop by ample teaspoonfuls into oil.
8. Fry to golden brown, turning once.
9. Drain on paper towels until lukewarm.
10. Roll in your choice of powdered sugar, sugar, or cinnamon and sugar; our family likes all three.

Waffles

My mom used to make us homemade waffles with her waffle iron. They are great plain, or with your favorite syrup, or add your choice of fruit or berries for a nice variation.

Ingredients:

1½ c. flour
3 tsp. baking powder
½ tsp. salt
2 Tbs. brown sugar
1½ c. buttermilk
3 egg yolks, beaten
6 Tbs. butter, melted
3 egg whites
1 c. your favorite fruit, finely chopped
   additional fruit for topping
   sweetened whipped cream

Directions:

1. In large bowl, sift together flour, baking powder, and salt.
2. In small bowl, combine egg yolks, buttermilk, and butter.
3. Beat in flour mixture; mix well.
4. In small bowl, beat egg whites until stiff.
5. Add brown sugar and beat again.
6. Gently fold into batter.
7. Gently stir in 1 cup fruit.
8. Grease waffle irons well and preheat to very hot.
9. Bake waffles until done.
10. Keep waffles in a warm oven while making the rest of them.
11. Serve with fruit topping and/or sweetened whipped cream.

Caramel Pecan Rolls

My mom used to make these for a special breakfast treat, and they are definitely one of our family's favorites. They freeze well, so you may think about doubling the recipe. Try the "do ahead" version if you are limited in time on the day you would like to make them.

Ingredients for caramel pecan topping:

    1 c. brown sugar, packed
    ½ c. butter, softened
    ¼ c. corn syrup
    1 c. pecan halves

Ingredients for filling:

    1 c. pecans, chopped
    ½ c. raisins
    ¼ c. sugar, granulated or brown, packed
    1 tsp. ground cinnamon

Ingredients for rolls:

    4 c. flour
    ⅓ c. sugar
    1 tsp. salt
    2 pkg. active dry yeast
    1 c. milk, very warm
    ¼ c. butter, softened
    1 lg. egg
    2 Tbs. butter
    extra butter

Directions for caramel pecan topping:

1. In 2-quart saucepan, heat brown sugar and butter to boiling, stirring constantly.

2. Remove from heat; stir in corn syrup.
3. Pour into ungreased 9 x 13 x 2-inch baking pan.
4. Sprinkle with pecan halves.

Directions for filling:

1. In small bowl, combine pecans, raisins, sugar, and cinnamon; set aside until ready to use.

Directions for rolls:

1. In large bowl, mix sugar, salt, yeast, and 2 cups flour.
2. Add warm milk, ¼ cup butter, and egg.
3. With electric mixer on low speed, beat 1 minute, scraping bowl frequently.
4. Stir in enough remaining flour to make dough easy to handle.
5. Place dough in large bowl greased with extra butter, turning dough to grease all sides.
6. Cover bowl loosely with plastic wrap; let dough rise in warm place, 1½ hours or until double in size.
7. Gently push fist into dough to deflate and remove from bowl to floured surface.
8. Pat, or roll dough into a 15 x 10-inch rectangle.
9. Spread with 2 tablespoons butter; sprinkle with filling.
10. Roll rectangle up tightly, beginning at long side.
11. Pinch edge of dough into roll to seal.
12. Cut roll into fifteen 1-inch slices using a sharp serrated knife.
13. Place slightly apart in pan on top of caramel pecan topping.
14. Cover loosely with plastic wrap; let rise in warm place 30 minutes, or until double in bulk.
15. Preheat oven to 350 degrees F.
16. Bake 30 to 35 minutes, or until golden brown.

17. Let stand 2 to 3 minutes; immediately turn upside down onto heatproof tray or serving plate.
18. Let stand upside down 1 minute so caramel can drizzle over rolls.
19. Remove pan; scrape any remaining syrup in bottom over the rolls; serve warm.

Directions for optional do-ahead rolls:

1. After placing slices in pan, cover tightly with plastic wrap or aluminum foil and refrigerate 4 to 24 hours.
2. Before baking, remove from refrigerator and let rise in warm place until double in size.
3. Proceed from number 7 on previous page.

Cheesy Scrambled Eggs

Our family loves scrambled eggs but only when they are made with plenty of melted cheese.

Ingredients:

8   lg. eggs
4   Tbs. butter
⅛ tsp. pepper
¼ c. milk
1½ c. Cheddar, Colby, or your favorite cheese, grated

Directions:

1. In medium bowl, add eggs, salt, and milk; beat well.
2. In frying pan, over medium-low heat, melt butter.
3. Add eggs and cheese.
4. Stir occasionally with spatula, turning eggs until cooked to soft-set stage when they have begun to firm up. When they begin to separate from the pan, you should remove them.
5. Serve with toast, biscuits, or croissants.

Swedish Pancakes

This is another breakfast favorite. These Swedish-style pancakes are great rolled up with just a dusting of powdered sugar. Serve with Swedish lingon berries if you like.

Ingredients:

    5 eggs
    2 c. milk
    1 c. flour
    ¾ tsp. salt
    ¼ c. butter, melted
    10 Tbs. butter

Ingredients for topping:

    powdered sugar

Directions:

1. In large bowl, beat eggs until light and fluffy.
2. Beat in milk.
3. Sift in flour and salt; beat until smooth.
4. Add melted butter; beat until well blended.
5. Prepare pancakes one at a time by melting 1 tablespoon butter in 9 or 10-inch skillet.
6. Add just enough batter to lightly cover bottom of skillet.
7. Tip skillet so batter covers the bottom of pan evenly.
8. Fry until golden brown on both sides, turning once.
9. Roll up and sprinkle with powdered sugar.
10. They are also delicious served hot with butter and syrup.

Yields: 10 servings.

Cheese Omelet

These cheese omelets are a favorite with my daughters who are vegetarian, and they are easy to make for the rest of the family, also. If you would like to add more flavors, try green onions, fresh tomatoes, mushrooms, or sun-dried tomatoes.

Ingredients:

    4 eggs
    4 tsp. butter
    ½ c. Cheddar cheese, shredded
        salt and pepper, to taste

Directions:

1. In small bowl, beat eggs with fork or wire whisk until well mixed.
2. In 8-inch skillet, over medium-high heat, add butter. Melt until butter is hot and sizzling.
3. As butter melts, tilt skillet to coat bottom with butter.
4. Quickly pour eggs into skillet.
5. While rapidly sliding skillet back and forth over heat, quickly stir eggs with a fork to spread them continuously over the bottom of the skillet as they thicken.
6. Let stand over heat a few seconds to lightly brown bottom of omelet. The omelet will continue to cook after being folded, so do not over cook.
7. Tilt skillet and run a spatula under edge of omelet, then jerk skillet sharply to loosen omelet from bottom of skillet.
8. Sprinkle with cheese.
9. Fold portion of omelet nearest you, just to the center. Allow for a portion of the omelet to slide up the side of skillet.

10. Turn omelet onto warm plate, flipping folded portion of omelet over so far side is on bottom, tucking sides of omelet under if desired.
11. Sprinkle with salt and pepper.
12. This is also delicious with a scoop of sour cream or salsa on the top.

Yields: 2 servings.

Mom's Special Omelet

This is a favorite in our household, and it is a great way to liven up a special weekend breakfast.

Ingredients:

6 eggs
4 slices of cheese
¾ c. mushrooms, sliced
4 Tbs. green onion, chopped
4 Tbs. red and yellow bell peppers, diced
4 Tbs. tomatoes, diced
½ c. ground sausage, cooked

Directions:

1. In small bowl, add eggs. Whisk with a fork; pour into a hot oiled skillet.
2. Cook eggs until almost done all the way through, then place prepared vegetables on top along with cooked sausage.
3. Place cheese over meat and vegetables; fold omelet in half.
4. Turn flame off and let cheeses melt all the way through before serving.
5. Serve immediately.

Yields: 2 servings.

Swiss Cheese and Mushroom Quiche

This is an easy-to-make quiche that is perfect for a late breakfast, or a brunch dish. You may vary the dish as preferred by substituting 1 cup of chopped scallions for the onion or using Cheddar cheese for Swiss cheese, or using fresh tomato slices instead of mushrooms.

Ingredients for quiche:

> 1½ c. Swiss cheese, grated
> 1   sm. onion, finely chopped
> ¼   lb. mushrooms, finely chopped
> 4   eggs
> 1½ c. milk
> 3   Tbs. flour
> ¼   tsp. salt
> ¼   tsp. dry mustard
>   paprika
>   butter
>   salt and pepper, to taste
>   thyme

Ingredients for pie crust:

> 1½ c. flour
> ¼   c. butter, chilled, cut into 1-inch cubes
> ¼   c. solid vegetable shortening, chilled
> ¼   tsp. salt
> ¼   c. cold water
>   flour, for your surface

Directions for pie crust:

1. Preheat oven to 400 degrees F.
2. In a mixer, blender, or food processor, blend flour, butter, and shortening until mixture is crumbly and the size of small peas.

3. Add liquid and mix until dough comes clean from bowl and forms a ball.
4. Flatten dough into 8-inch circle; enclose in plastic wrap and place in refrigerator for at least 30 minutes.
5. Place dough on lightly floured surface.
6. Roll dough into a 12-inch circle and dust lightly with flour.
7. Place rolling pin at edge of circle of dough, and roll dough up onto and around rolling pin.
8. Gently unroll dough from rolling pin into a greased pie pan.
9. Without forcing or stretching dough, press into pan.
10. Allow 1 inch to overhang on pan, trim excess.
11. Roll 1 inch overhanging dough under for thin roll.
12. Pinch edges between thumb and forefinger every inch for an attractive edge.
13. Prick sides and bottom with fork.
14. Line with wax paper; fill with raw rice or beans and then bake 25 minutes.
15. Remove paper with beans or rice and cook another 5 minutes or so.

Directions for filling:

1. Preheat oven to 375 degrees F.
2. Cover bottom of crust with cheese.
3. In small skillet, sauté onions and mushrooms in butter with salt, pepper, and thyme.
4. Cover cheese with sautéed onion and mushrooms.
5. In small bowl, beat together eggs, milk, flour, dry mustard, and ¼ teaspoon of salt to make custard.
6. Pour custard over mushroom and onion layer.
7. Sprinkle with paprika.
8. Bake 40 to 45 minutes, or until solid in center when jiggled.
9. Remove from oven; let stand a few minutes.
10. Cut into wedges while hot.
11. Serve immediately.

Eggs Benedict with Hollandaise Sauce

This is an enjoyable classic and is easier to make than expected. The trick is to have everything ready and make all items at the same time.

Ingredients for Hollandaise sauce:

> 5 egg yolks
> 5 tsp. cold water
> ¾ c. butter, softened
> ¼ tsp. salt
> 1 tsp. lemon juice, or to taste

Ingredients for eggs:

> 8 slices Canadian bacon
> 4 English muffins, halved
> 1 tsp. butter
> 8 eggs
> 8 truffle slices (optional)

Directions for Hollandaise sauce:

1. In top of double boiler, combine egg yolks and water.
2. Beat with a wire whisk over hot, not boiling, water until fluffy.
3. Stir in a few spoonfuls of butter to the mixture.
4. Beat continually until the butter has melted and the sauce starts to thicken.
5. Care should be taken that the water in the bottom of the boiler never boils.
6. Continue adding butter, bit by bit, stirring constantly.
7. Add salt and lemon juice; stir.
8. For a lighter texture, beat in a tablespoon of hot water if desired.

Directions for eggs benedict:

1. In small skillet, sauté bacon briefly in butter, and keep hot.
2. Meanwhile, poach eggs in boiling water.
3. Place each slice of bacon on a toasted English muffin half that has been lightly buttered.
4. Top each bacon slice with a poached egg.
5. Cover with Hollandaise sauce.
6. If desired, garnish with a truffle slice.

Yields: 8 servings.

Easy Soufflé

This is a simple to make and quick soufflé that is simply scrumptious.

Ingredients:

1¼ c. Cheddar cheese, sharp, cubed (10 oz.)
1 tsp. salt
10 slices bread, buttered, cubed
4 eggs
2 c. milk
1 tsp. French cream mustard, or ½ tsp. dry mustard

Directions:

1. Preheat oven to 350 degrees F.
2. Lightly grease a 1½-quart casserole dish.
3. In blender container, combine cheese, salt, bread, mustard, and eggs; blend on high speed until thoroughly mixed.
4. Add milk and blend well; pour into prepared dish.
5. Bake uncovered, 1 hour.
6. Serve immediately, as letting it set will deflate the soufflé.

Eggs Benedict–Classic Style

Our family enjoys eggs. This recipe works very well for those on a low-carb diet.

Ingredients for eggs:

    3 Tbs. white vinegar
    1 tsp. salt
       eggs, room temperature
       water

Ingredients for Hollandaise sauce:

    6 egg yolks
    2 Tbs. cold water
    1 c. butter, softened
    ½ tsp. salt
    1 tsp. lemon juice, or to taste

Directions:

1. Add 1 inch of water to a skillet; add vinegar and salt. Bring to boil; reduce heat immediately.
2. Break eggs one at a time into a saucer; slip gently into boiled water.
3. Let eggs steep until the whites are firm.
4. Remove eggs; drain on paper towels. Trim with a knife or cookie cutter.

Directions for Hollandaise sauce:

1. In top of double boiler, combine egg yolks and water; beat with wire whisk over hot, not boiling, water until fluffy.
2. Add a few spoonfuls of butter to mixture; beat continually until butter has melted and sauce starts to thicken. Don't let water boil in bottom of boiler.
3. Continue adding butter, bit by bit, stirring constantly, until all has been added and melted.
4. Add salt and lemon juice. For a lighter texture, beat in a tablespoon of hot water if desired.
5. If making a large amount, reheat poached eggs in boiling, salted water 30 seconds, just before serving.

Mother's Day Delights Cookbook
A Collection of Mother's Day Recipes
Cookbook Delights Holiday Series-Book 5

Cakes

Table of Contents

Page

Chocolate Velvet Cake

This is a very moist and easy-to-make chocolate cake.
Mayonnaise is used instead of oil to add that bit of extra
moisture which makes the cake like velvet in your mouth.

Ingredients:

2¼ c. flour
1 tsp. baking soda
¼ tsp. baking powder
1⅓ c. sugar
3 eggs
1 tsp. vanilla extract
1 c. mayonnaise
4 sq. unsweetened chocolate, melted
1⅓ c. water

Directions:

1. Preheat oven to 350 degrees F.
2. Grease and flour a 9 x 13-inch baking pan.
3. In large bowl, sift together flour, baking soda, and baking powder; set aside.
4. In large bowl, with electric mixer at high speed, beat sugar, eggs, and vanilla for 3 minutes, or until fluffy.
5. Reduce speed to low; beat in mayonnaise and chocolate until well blended.
6. Continuing at low speed, add flour mixture in 4 additions alternately with water, beating just until blended after each addition.
7. Spoon into prepared pan.
8. Bake 45 minutes, or until inserted toothpick in center comes out clean.
9. Cool completely in pan.
10. Ice or frost with your favorite frosting.

Angel Cake Supreme

This is a delicious, classic angel cake. Serve it plain, frosted, or with fruit and whipped cream for a delightful dessert.

Ingredients:

    1   c. cake flour, sifted
    1¼ c. powdered sugar, sifted
    12 egg whites
    1½ tsp. cream of tartar
    ¼   tsp. salt
    1½ tsp. vanilla extract
    ¼   tsp. almond extract
    1   c. sugar

Directions:

1. Preheat oven to 375 degrees F.
2. In medium bowl, sift flour with powdered sugar 3 times.
3. In large bowl, beat egg whites with cream of tartar, salt, vanilla, and almond extract until stiff enough to hold up in soft peaks but still moist and glossy.
4. Gradually beat in sugar, 2 tablespoons at a time; continue to beat until the meringue holds stiff peaks.
5. Sift ¼ of the flour mixture over whites; lightly fold in by hand, using a "down, up, and over" motion, turning the bowl with each fold.
6. Fold in remaining flour by fourths.
7. Spoon into an ungreased 10-inch tube pan.
8. Bake 30 minutes, or until no indentation when lightly touched on top.
9. Remove from oven; invert pan and cool cake thoroughly.
10. Loosen sides of cake from pan and turn onto cake plate.
11. Remove bottom tube.
12. Frost or serve as desired.

German Apple Cake

This is a great-tasting, moist cake that can be made ahead of time and also freezes well unfrosted.

Ingredients for cake:

3	eggs
1	c. canola oil
2	c. sugar
2	c. flour
2	Tbs. cinnamon
1	tsp. baking soda
4½	c. apples, peeled, thinly sliced
1½	c. nuts, chopped

Ingredients for frosting:

1	c. cream cheese
1	tsp. vanilla extract
3	Tbs. butter
1½	c. powdered sugar
	food coloring, if desired

Directions for cake:

1. Preheat oven to 350 degrees F.
2. Grease and flour a 9 x13-inch baking pan.
3. In large bowl, beat eggs and oil until foamy.
4. Add sugar, flour, cinnamon, and baking soda; blend until smooth.
5. Fold in apples and nuts until mixed.
6. Pour into prepared pan.
7. Bake 50 to 60 minutes.
8. Turn out onto wire rack to cool.

Directions for frosting:

1. In medium bowl, with electric mixer, combine cream cheese, vanilla, butter, and powdered sugar; beat well.

2. Add food coloring if desired.
3. Spread over cooled cake.

Jewish Apple Cake

This is a substantial cake that is delicious as well as filling, so you might choose to serve it as a later snack after your main meal.

Ingredients:

2¾ c. sugar
1 tsp. cinnamon
4 c. flour
1 tsp. salt
4 tsp. baking powder
1 c. orange juice
4 eggs
1 c. canola oil
5 apples, peeled, cored, sliced

Directions:

1. Preheat oven to 350 degrees F.
2. Lightly grease a bundt pan.
3. In small bowl, mix ¾ cup of sugar with cinnamon; set aside.
4. In large bowl, sift together flour, remaining sugar, salt, and baking powder.
5. Make well in center.
6. Add orange juice, eggs, and oil; beat well.
7. Pour half the batter into prepared pan.
8. Spread half the apple slices over top; sprinkle with half the sugar-cinnamon mixture.
9. Cover with remaining batter; top with remaining apples and sprinkle with remaining sugar-cinnamon mixture.
10. Bake 1½ hours, or until inserted toothpick in center comes out clean.
11. Turn out onto wire rack to cool.

American Fudge Cake

*My son Caleb loves chocolate and often requests this
very rich chocolate fudge cake for his birthday.*

Ingredients for cake:

½ c. butter
1 c. dark brown sugar
2 eggs
½ c. sour cream
¾ c. flour
1 tsp. baking powder
½ tsp. baking soda
¼ c. cocoa

Ingredients for filling:

2 Tbs. cocoa
2 Tbs. boiling water
½ c. butter
⅔ c. powdered sugar, sifted
vanilla essence

Ingredients for frosting:

1 c. sweetened chocolate, broken into pieces
2 Tbs. cocoa
2 Tbs. boiling water
½ c. cream

Directions for cake:

1. Preheat oven to 375 degrees F.
2. Butter and flour two 8-inch baking pans.
3. In medium bowl, cream butter and sugar until light
   and fluffy.

4. Gradually beat in eggs and sour cream. The mixture will look curdled at this stage.
5. In large bowl, sift together flour, baking powder, baking soda, and cocoa; fold into egg mixture.
6. Divide mixture equally between prepared pans.
7. Bake 30 to 35 minutes, or until inserted toothpick in center comes out clean.
8. Turn out onto wire rack to cool.
9. Place in freezer while making filling.

Directions for filling:

1. In small bowl, mix cocoa with water to a smooth paste; cool.
2. In medium bowl, cream butter, powdered sugar, and vanilla essence until light and fluffy.
3. Beat in cocoa paste.
4. Slice cake in half horizontally; place one half on a serving plate; spread the halves with filling and stack on top of each other until all four layers are on the plate.

Directions for frosting:

1. In small microwave-safe bowl, melt chocolate in microwave.
2. In small bowl, make cocoa into a paste with water as before; mix with the melted chocolate.
3. Slowly whisk cream into chocolate until smooth and thickened.
4. Spread frosting evenly over the cake.
5. Serve warm in slices, with ice cream.

Did You Know? . . . .

Did you know that tradition calls for the wearing of carnations on Mother's Day? A red one if one's mother is alive, and white if she has died.

Carrot Cake

This is a delicious moist cake that is always enjoyed. It keeps well and freezes well. If you like, add raisins to this cake for a change of pace.

Ingredients for cake:

  4 eggs
  1 c. canola oil
  1 c. cream cheese
  1 Tbs. vanilla extract
  2 c. flour
  2 c. sugar
  2 tsp. baking powder
  1 tsp. baking soda
  ½ tsp. salt
  2 tsp. cinnamon
  1 c. walnuts, chopped
  3 c. raw carrots, grated

Ingredients for cream cheese frosting:

  ½ c. butter
  1 c. cream cheese
  1 tsp. vanilla extract
  1 lb. powdered sugar, sifted

Directions for cake:

1. Preheat oven to 350 degrees F.
2. Grease and flour a 9 x 13-inch baking.
3. In large bowl, beat together eggs, oil, and cream cheese; add vanilla.
4. In large bowl, sift together flour, sugar, baking powder, baking soda, salt, and cinnamon; add to egg mixture and beat until well blended.
5. Fold in walnuts and grated carrots; mix well.
6. Pour batter into prepared pan.
7. Bake 40 to 45 minutes, or until inserted toothpick comes out clean.

8. Turn out onto wire rack to cool.

Directions for cream cheese frosting:

1. In small bowl, beat butter and cream cheese together until well blended.
2. Add vanilla and sugar; beat until smooth.

Rhubarb Buttermilk Cake

This is an easy-to-make rhubarb cake.

Ingredients:

1½ c. brown sugar
½ c. butter
1 tsp. vanilla extract
2 c. flour
1 tsp. baking soda
½ tsp. salt
1 egg, slightly beaten
1 c. buttermilk
1½ c. rhubarb, chopped
½ c. sugar
1 tsp. cinnamon

Directions:

1. Preheat oven to 350 degrees F.
2. Lightly grease and flour a 9 x 13-inch baking pan.
3. In large bowl, cream butter, sugar, egg, milk, and vanilla.
4. In small bowl, combine flour, baking soda, and salt.
5. Add dry ingredients to butter mixture.
6. Fold in rhubarb; pour into prepared baking pan.
7. In small bowl, combine sugar and cinnamon.
8. Spread on top of cake.
9. Bake 50 minutes, or until inserted toothpick in center comes out clean.

Fun Cake

Like its name says, this is a fun cake to make. The frosting is light, fluffy, and delicious.

Ingredients for cake:

1½ c. flour
1   c. sugar
1   tsp. baking soda
½   tsp. salt
3   Tbs. cocoa
1   tsp. vanilla extract
1   Tbs. vinegar
5   Tbs. olive oil
1   c. cold water

Ingredients for frosting:

2   egg whites
¾   c. sugar
⅓   c. light corn syrup
2   Tbs. water
¼   tsp. salt
¼   tsp. cream of tartar
2   drops food coloring, your choice
½   tsp. vanilla extract, or your favorite
    your choice of toppings: nuts, coconut, chocolate
    chips, candy coated chocolates, gummi candies

Directions for cake:

1. Preheat oven to 350 degrees F.
2. In bottom of a flat, ungreased baking pan, sift flour, sugar, baking soda, salt, and cocoa together; make three indentations in mixture.
3. Into one, put vanilla.
4. Into the second, put vinegar.
5. Into the third, put oil.
6. Over the whole mixture, pour 1 cup of cold water.
7. Beat in pan until smooth.

8. Bake 35 minutes.
9. Cool 10 minutes.
10. Turn upside down on wire rack to cool.

Directions for frosting:

1. In top of double boiler, combine all ingredients except flavoring and coloring; beat well.
2. Place over bottom of double boiler on medium heat.
3. Continue beating with electric mixer until mixture stands in peaks.
4. Fold in flavoring and coloring; beat until light and fluffy.
5. Frost cake and top with your favorite toppings.

Rhubarb Shortcake

This is an easy-to-make shortcake. Serve with sweetened whipped cream or homemade ice cream.

Ingredients for rhubarb:

4   c. rhubarb, chopped
1½ c. sugar
2   Tbs. butter

Ingredients for shortcake batter:

1   egg
½   c. milk
½   c. sugar
1   c. flour
1   tsp. baking powder

Directions for both:

1. Preheat oven to 350 degrees F.
2. In large bowl, mix rhubarb, sugar, and butter.
3. Turn into a 9 x 13-inch baking pan.
4. In medium bowl, mix batter and pour over rhubarb.
5. Bake 1 hour, or until done.

Grandma Bert's Quick Cake

Grandma Bert used to make this cake as a treat for our family when she came to visit. It is easy to make and very delicious.

Ingredients for cake:

2   eggs
3   Tbs. butter, melted
1   c. sugar
1   tsp. baking powder
1   c. flour
½   tsp. salt
2   tsp. vanilla extract
½   c. milk, heated

Ingredients for frosting:

⅓   c. butter, melted
¾   c. brown sugar, firmly packed
⅓   c. light or half and half cream
1½ c. nuts, chopped
2   c. coconut, flaked or shredded

Directions for cake:

1. Preheat oven to 350 degrees F.
2. Grease and flour a 9-inch square baking pan.
3. In medium bowl, beat eggs until thick and light colored; add melted butter and beat again.
4. In medium bowl, sift together sugar, flour, baking powder, and salt; add to egg mixture.
5. Fold in hot milk and vanilla.
6. Pour into prepared pan.
7. Bake 25 to 30 minutes, or until inserted toothpick in center comes out clean.
8. Place on wire rack, in pan, to cool.

Directions for broiled frosting:

1. In small bowl, combine butter, sugar, and cream.
2. Spread mixture over cake; add nuts and coconut.
3. Place under broiler and broil for a few minutes.

Blueberry Coconut Pound Cake

This recipe can be made as a pound cake or muffins. It is moist and delicious.

Ingredients:

½ c. butter, softened
¾ c. sugar
2 tsp. lime zest, freshly grated
5 Tbs. heavy cream
¾ c. blueberries
¾ c. coconut, sweetened, flaked
1 c. flour
2 lg. eggs

Directions:

1. Preheat oven to 350 degrees F.; put rack in middle.
2. Grease or paper-line 7 to 9 half-cup muffin cups.
3. In large bowl, with electric mixer, beat butter, sugar, and zest until light and fluffy.
4. Beat in eggs, one at a time.
5. Add cream and flour; mix on low speed until just combined.
6. Stir in ½ cup of coconut; gently stir in blueberries.
7. Spoon batter into cups until almost full; smooth tops.
8. Sprinkle tops with remaining coconut.
9. Bake 25 minutes, or until inserted toothpick in center comes out clean with edges golden.
10. Invert on wire rack and cool.

Raspberry Bavarian Cake

This is a very refreshing pudding-style cake which is molded, then sliced after setting.

Ingredients:

    1½ Tbs. unflavored gelatin
    ¼ c. cold water
    2   c. milk
    2   eggs, separated
    ¾ c. sugar
    1   tsp. lemon juice
    1   c. fresh raspberries
    ½ c. heavy cream, whipped
    ½ c. fresh raspberries for garnish

Directions:

1. In small cup, soften gelatin in cold water for 5 minutes.
2. In small saucepan, scald milk; add gelatin mixture, and stir until dissolved.
3. In small bowl, mix egg yolks with sugar; gradually add hot milk.
4. In top of double boiler, cook over boiling water, 3 minutes, or until mixture coats a spoon.
5. Remove from heat and chill.
6. While chilling, as mixture begins to thicken, add lemon juice and raspberries.
7. In medium bowl, beat egg whites until stiff, and fold into chilled raspberry mixture along with whipped cream.
8. Pour mixture into springform pan and chill in refrigerator until firm.
9. Remove from refrigerator; unmold and cut into slices.
10. Garnish with fresh raspberries.

Mother's Day Delights Cookbook
A Collection of Mother's Day Recipes
Cookbook Delights Holiday Series-Book 5

Candies

Table of Contents

Page

Best Fudge Recipe

This fudge recipe is the best one I've tried. It is creamy with great tasting chocolate, packed with walnuts. Try using milk chocolate or dark chocolate to suit your taste. This is another family favorite recipe.

Ingredients:

2¼ c. top quality chocolate chips, room temperature
3   c. walnuts, chopped in lg. pieces
1   can evaporated milk
1   jar marshmallow crème, room temperature (9 oz.)
3   tsp. vanilla extract
½   lb. butter, room temperature
4½ c. sugar
    extra butter

Directions:

1. Butter a 9 x 13-inch baking pan; cover with wax paper. Butter wax paper as well.
2. In large bowl, combine all ingredients, except milk and sugar.
3. In large saucepan, combine milk and sugar.
4. Bring to rolling boil; reduce heat.
5. Boil on low for 11 minutes, stirring constantly with wooden spoon. It may turn brown, so don't be alarmed.
6. Pour mixture over ingredients in large bowl.
7. Mix quickly but do not beat.
8. Pour into prepared pan.
9. Important: Get it out of bowl and into pan as rapidly as possible.
10. Chill slightly; cut into small squares.
11. Note: Do not make substitutions as it may not turn out as well.

Molasses Taffy

This is a fun project for children and moms to make together.

Ingredients:

 2 c. sugar
 1 c. light molasses
 ¼ c. water
 2 tsp. vinegar
 2 Tbs. butter
 ½ tsp. baking soda

Directions:

1. Butter sides of heavy 2-quart saucepan.
2. In saucepan, combine sugar, molasses, and water.
3. Heat slowly, stirring constantly until sugar is dissolved; bring to boil, add vinegar, and cook to light-crack stage.
4. Remove from heat; add butter and sift in baking soda; stir to mix.
5. Turn out (don't scrape) onto buttered platter or large shallow pan.
6. For even cooling, use a spatula to turn the edges to the center.
7. When taffy is just cool enough to handle, cut into long lengths and pull.
8. Use only finger tips to pull – if candy sticks, dip fingers in cornstarch.
9. Pull candy into long ropes, doubling back over into itself as you pull and continue pulling until it can no longer be pulled or starts breaking.
10. Cut each rope into 2-inch pieces and wrap individually or store pieces between sheets of wax paper in an airtight container.

Blobs

These were one of my favorite sweet treats when I was a child. My aunt used to make them for me and they were a hit when I brought them to group meetings for children.

Ingredients:

    1 c. white corn syrup
    1 c. sugar
    7 c. crispy rice cereal
    1 c. creamy peanut butter
    1 c. butter
    1 c. butterscotch chips
    1 c. chocolate chips

Directions:

1. Generously butter a 9 x 13-inch baking pan.
2. In large saucepan, bring syrup and sugar just to a boil.
3. Add peanut butter to hot syrup; add cereal.
4. Mix well.
5. In small saucepan, melt butter, butterscotch and chocolate chips.
6. Pour over cereal mixture; mix well.
7. Drop by spoonfuls or spread into prepared pan.

Peach Candy Chews

These peach candies are a delicious favorite for a special treat. You may also use apricots or a combination of both if preferred.

Ingredients:

    4   fresh peaches, peeled, diced
    ⅓ c. water
    3¾ c. sugar
    2   Tbs. unflavored gelatin

2   tsp. lemon peel, grated
1   Tbs. lemon juice
    canola oil
    sugar

Directions:

1. Lightly grease a 9-inch square pan.
2. In 6-quart saucepan, combine peaches and water; over high heat, bring to boil, stirring constantly.
3. Reduce heat to medium, cover and simmer 10 to 12 minutes, stirring occasionally, until peaches mash easily; cool.
4. In blender, process fruit mixture a portion at a time, until smoothly puréed, then return to pan.
5. In medium bowl, mix 3½ cups sugar with gelatin; stir into fruit mixture.
6. Over medium-high heat, bring to boil.
7. Boil 5 minutes.
8. Reduce heat to medium-low, stirring constantly, until mixture thickens and does not run together when the spoon is drawn through the fruit on bottom of pan; cook 25 to 30 minutes, or until juices are a light brown color.
9. Remove peach mixture from heat.
10. Stir in lemon peel and lemon juice.
11. Spoon peach mixture into prepared baking pan.
12. Let candy dry, uncovered, until it feels firm and not sticky when touched, about 16 to 24 hours.
13. Coat work surface with sugar.
14. Invert pan to release candy onto sugar covered area. If candy sticks, use a spatula, dipped in sugar, to ease from pan.
15. With a sharp knife, dipped in sugar to prevent sticking, cut candy into equal pieces of desired size.
16. Turn each piece over and coat completely with sugar.
17. Candies may be wrapped individually or arranged in a container with plastic wrap between layers and sealed airtight.
18. Will keep up to 1 month at room temperature.

Candy Krispies

*These are simply the same type of crispy marshmallow
and cereal bar treats that we have all known for years, but
with the addition of candies. Easy to make, and fun to eat.*

Ingredients:

½ c. butter
33 lg. marshmallows or 3 c. miniature marshmallows
5 c. rice cereal
1 c. your favorite candy pieces, chopped small
    extra butter

Directions:

1. Butter a 9 x 13-inch baking pan.
2. In 4-quart saucepan, melt butter and marshmallows.
3. Add rice cereal and candy pieces.
4. Quickly mix the whole mixture well; place in prepared pan; spread with a buttered spatula.
5. Place in refrigerator to chill; cut into squares.

English Toffee Pan-Fried

*This toffee is super easy to make and very tasty. The
trick is to brown the toffee to the perfect caramelized color.
Use your favorite milk chocolate or dark chocolate.*

Ingredients:

2 Tbs. light corn syrup
1 c. butter
1 c. sugar
1 c. chocolate chips
1 c. walnut, chopped
  extra butter

Directions:

1. Lightly butter a baking sheet; sprinkle with nuts.
2. In large skillet, over high heat, place corn syrup, butter, and sugar.
3. Cook, stirring constantly, until light brown colored.
4. Pour onto prepared baking sheet.
5. Let candy stand for 2 to 3 minutes.
6. Cover candy with chocolate chips.
7. Let candy stand until chocolate is melted.
8. Spread chocolate evenly.
9. When chocolate is hardened, score top and break into pieces.
10. Store in tightly covered container between sheets of wax paper.

Peanut Butter Coconut Candy

This is a quick-to-fix treat that is not too sweet, and easily stored.

Ingredients:

1 pkg. butterscotch chips, melted (12 oz.)
6 Tbs. peanut butter
4 c. corn flakes
2 c. coconut

Directions:

1. Lightly butter a 9 x 13-inch baking pan.
2. In large bowl, mix melted butterscotch chips with peanut butter.
3. Add corn flakes and coconut.
4. Mix all together; pat into prepared pan.
5. When firm, cut into squares and serve.

Chocolate Raspberry Truffles

The most beloved of French candies, the truffle is fast becoming one of America's favorites too. Our version has an optional cocoa powder dusting, (although in France, it is considered by many to be a requirement!) or a crunchy hazelnut outer coating.

Ingredients:

¾ c. butter
1 lb. quality semi-sweet chocolate, finely chopped
½ c. seedless raspberry jam
¼ c. black raspberry liqueur or raspberry chambord
½ c. Dutch process cocoa powder
1 c. hazelnuts, roasted, finely chopped

Directions:

1. Cut butter into pieces and melt in top of double boiler or metal bowl over (but not touching) hot water.
2. Add chocolate, stirring occasionally until smooth.
3. Remove from heat.
4. Blend in raspberry jam and raspberry liqueur until smooth.
5. Cover; freeze 2 hours, until firm, or refrigerate 4 hours, until firm, or overnight.
6. Place cocoa or hazelnuts in a wide, shallow pie pan.
7. Using a melon baller or a tablespoon, scoop a tablespoon of cold chocolate mixture between your palms and roll to form a round ball.
8. Roll in desired coating and place on a sided baking sheet. Repeat until all the chocolate mixture is gone.
9. Cover tightly with plastic wrap and refrigerate until ready to serve. Remove from refrigerator 10 minutes before serving.

10. Note: This recipe may be prepared up to 5 days
    ahead if truffles are covered tightly and refrigerated.
11. They may also be frozen for up to a month, double
    wrapped in plastic.

Salt Water Taffy

*This taffy is fun to make and very tasty. Children and
adults alike have fun making this together.*

Ingredients:

    2 tsp. butter
    1 c. sugar
    ⅔ c. water
    ¾ c. light corn syrup
    1 Tbs. cornstarch
    1 tsp. salt
    2 tsp. butter
    1 tsp. strawberry flavoring

Directions:

1. Grease an 8 x 8 x 2-inch pan with 2 teaspoons
    butter.
2. In small saucepan, combine sugar, water, corn
    syrup, cornstarch, and salt.
3. Cook over medium heat, stirring occasionally, until
    candy thermometer reads 256 degrees F.
4. Remove from heat at once.
5. Stir in desired flavoring and pour into prepared pan.
6. Allow candy to cool just enough to handle.
7. Cut candy into strips and then pull each taffy strip
    until it is light in color and stiff.
8. Pull into 2-inch strips, cut, and wrap in wax paper.

Yields: 1 pound candy.

Divinity

My mom used to make this divinity candy on holidays and special occasions. She would make pink divinity with nuts for Valentine's Day, but you may change the color and fruit and nuts to match your special occasion.

Ingredients:

2½ c. sugar
½ c. light corn syrup
½ c. water
2   egg whites, stiffly beaten
1   tsp. vanilla extract
½ c. candied fruit or nuts, chopped
2   drops of red food coloring

Directions:

1. In heavy saucepan, mix sugar, corn syrup, and water.
2. Over medium-high heat, cook and stir until boiling.
3. Reduce heat to medium; cook without stirring, 10 to 15 minutes, until candy reaches hardball stage.
4. Remove from heat.
5. Gradually pour hot mixture in a thin stream over egg whites while beating on high for 3 minutes, scraping bowl as you beat mixture.
6. Add vanilla and, if desired, food coloring.
7. Continue beating on high just until candy starts to lose its gloss. When beaters are lifted, mixture should fall in a ribbon that mounds on itself. This final beating should take 5 to 6 minutes.
8. Immediately stir in fruits or nuts.
9. Quickly drop remaining mixture by teaspoonfuls onto wax paper.
10. If mixture flattens out, beat another ½ to 1 minute, then continue to spoon out.

11. If mixture is too stiff to spoon, beat in a few drops hot water until candy is a softer consistency.

Peanut Butter Fudge

Our family loves peanuts and peanut butter and this makes a creamy, wonderful treat.

Ingredients:

¼ c. roasted, unsalted peanuts, coarsely chopped
1   c. milk
2½ c. sugar
3   Tbs. butter
¾ c. creamy peanut butter
1   tsp. vanilla extract

Directions:

1. Line an 8 x 8-inch baking pan with aluminum foil and lightly grease with nonstick cooking spray.
2. Sprinkle the peanuts over the bottom of the pan.
3. Put the milk and sugar in a medium, heavy bottomed saucepan fitted with a candy thermometer.
4. Boil over medium heat, occasionally stirring to keep from sticking.
5. Cook until the mixture reaches 240 degrees F.
6. Remove from heat; gently place butter, peanut butter, and vanilla in the pan, taking care not to disturb the syrup. Do not stir.
7. Cool 5 minutes, then beat vigorously with a spoon or the flat beater of a stationary mixer until dense and smooth.
8. Turn fudge into prepared pan, spreading it evenly with a metal spatula.
9. Let set 45 minutes; cut into 1⅓-inch squares.

Cherry Almond Clusters

The combination of chocolate, almonds, and cherries makes this a delicious candy. It is a great homemade treat to send to loved ones far away. It travels well when packed tightly in a tin.

Ingredients:

> 1 c. semi-sweet baking chocolate
> 1 c. slivered almonds, toasted
> 1 c. dried cherries

Directions:

1. Preheat oven to 350 degrees F.
2. To toast almonds: Spread almonds on an ungreased baking sheet. Bake 5 to 7 minutes, stirring occasionally.
3. Put chocolate in a microwave-safe bowl.
4. Microwave on high for 2 minutes, stirring halfway through the heating time.
5. Stir again, until chocolate is completely melted.
6. Quickly add toasted almonds and dried cherries.
7. Mix until completely coated with chocolate.
8. Drop by teaspoonfuls onto wax paper.
9. Refrigerate until firm.

Homemade Pecan Caramels

Nothing is better than homemade for a chewy, creamy caramel, and we like ours with the addition of pecans.

Ingredients:

> 1 c. butter
> 2 c. brown sugar, firmly packed
> 1 tsp. vanilla extract
> 1 c. light corn syrup
> 1 can sweetened condensed milk

1 c. pecans, chopped
  extra butter

Directions:

1. Lightly butter a baking dish.
2. In large saucepan, combine butter, sugar, and corn syrup; mix well.
3. Over medium heat, stir continuously for 15 minutes.
4. Remove from heat; stir in pecans and vanilla.
5. Pour into prepared dish; refrigerate.
6. Chill 2 hours; cut into squares.
7. Store between sheets of wax paper in an airtight container in refrigerator.

Turtles

This recipe is from my sister Sandy. She liked making these for friends and family. They were always enjoyed by everyone.

Ingredients:

70 caramels
5 Tbs. cream
4½ c. pecans
2 giant milk chocolate bars
½ bar paraffin wax, cut into pieces

Directions:

1. In double boiler, melt caramels and cream; add pecans.
2. Drop mixture by teaspoonfuls onto a greased baking sheet and freeze.
3. In top of double boiler, over high heat, melt chocolate bars, adding paraffin wax pieces, stirring until all wax is melted.
4. Dip frozen candy into melted chocolate wax mixture and place on baking sheet.
5. Let set until chocolate coating is hardened.

Northwestern Apple Candy

This candy is very tasty, soft, and chewy with the combination of apples and nuts and then dusted with powdered sugar. This candy also makes a great homemade gift.

Ingredients:

    5 apples, unpeeled, washed, cut into sm. pieces
    2 Tbs. unflavored gelatin
    ½ c. cold water
    2 c. sugar
    1 Tbs. cornstarch
    ¼ tsp. salt
    ¾ c. walnuts, coarsely chopped
    1 tsp. lemon peel, grated
    1 Tbs. lemon juice
       powdered sugar

Directions:

1. In 2-quart heavy saucepan, place apples and salt.
2. Cook until tender, in just enough water to avoid scorching.
3. Place mixture in blender, purée, and measure 2 cups of pulp back into the saucepan.
4. Cook measured pulp until thickened, stirring often.
5. In small bowl, soften gelatin in cold water.
6. In small bowl, mix sugar and cornstarch together and add to apple pulp.
7. Cook again over low heat, stirring constantly, until mixture is thick.
8. Add gelatin mixture; stir until gelatin dissolves and mixture again thickens.
9. Remove from heat.
10. Stir in walnuts, lemon peel, and juice.

11. Turn into a 9 x 12-inch square, shallow, glass dish that has just been rinsed with cold water.
12. Let stand 24 hours.
13. Cut candy into 30 to 40 squares.
14. Roll each piece in powdered sugar and place on wire rack until outside is dry.
15. Store in covered container.

Huckleberry Cream Fudge

Huckleberry cream fudge is a great treat here in the Northwest. Enjoy this colorful, creamy fudge.

Ingredients:

2 c. sugar
1 c. light cream
1 Tbs. light corn syrup
½ tsp. salt
1 Tbs. butter
2 tsp. vanilla extract
¾ c. fresh huckleberries

Directions:

1. Lightly butter an 8 x 8-inch pan.
2. In heavy 2-quart saucepan, combine sugar, cream, corn syrup, and salt.
3. Bring to boil over moderate heat, stirring constantly; cook to 238 degrees F.
4. Remove from heat; cool to 110 degrees F. Do not stir.
5. Add butter and vanilla; beat with wooden spoon until mixture becomes very thick and loses its gloss.
6. Stir in huckleberries.
7. Spread into prepared pan.
8. Score squares while fudge is still warm.
9. Cut when cooled.

Peanut Butter Cups

These are some of my family favorites. The children especially love these homemade peanut butter cups.

Ingredients:

> 1½ lb. semi-sweet or bitter sweet chocolate or
> quality chocolate chips.
> ¾ c. semi-sweet or bitter-sweet chocolate, chopped
> 2   c. creamy peanut butter

Directions:

1. Melt 1 lb. chocolate and make your own chocolate cups, using mini paper cups that you will cover with chocolate, let set, smooth rims, and then remove the paper, or, if preferred, you may buy the ready made chocolate cups.
2. Melt the ¾ cup of chocolate; remove from heat and stir until smooth. Cool to warm room temperature.
3. Add peanut butter; stir with wooden spoon until thoroughly blended.
4. Spoon mixture into a sturdy resealable plastic bag and snip off the tip of one corner.
5. Pipe the mixture into the chocolate cups until it almost reaches the rims.
6. Tap cups lightly to release any air bubbles.
7. Let peanut butter cups stand in a cool, dry place for 1 hour or until set. The filling will be soft and creamy but will still hold its shape.
8. Melt remaining ½ pound chocolate.
9. Using a teaspoon, lightly coat tops of peanut butter mixture in each cup to seal.
10. Tap cups lightly to smooth chocolate slightly.
11. Note: The peanut butter cups may be refrigerated in an airtight container for up to a week.

Mother's Day Delights Cookbook
A Collection of Mother's Day Recipes
Cookbook Delights Holiday Series-Book 5

Cookies

Table of Contents

Page

German Sour Cream Twists

Grandma Bert has always made these to take as gifts for dinners and treats for others. They make a wonderful cookie to serve for special occasions such as Mother's Day. They are delicious either warm or cold.

Ingredients:

    2   whole eggs
    4   egg yolks
    7   c. flour
    2   tsp. salt
    1   c. shortening
    1   c. butter
    2   pkg. active dry yeast
    ½ c. water, very warm
    1½ c. sour cream
    2   tsp. vanilla extract
    2   c. sugar

Directions:

1. In small bowl, beat together whole eggs with additional egg yolks; set aside.
2. In large mixing bowl, combine flour and salt; cut in shortening and butter at the same time.
3. In small bowl, dissolve yeast in very warm water.
4. Combine yeast water with eggs, sour cream, and vanilla, stirring well to blend.
5. Add to flour mixture and scrape dough from sides of bowl; divide dough in half.
6. Cover and refrigerate for 2 hours.
7. Remove one of the halves at a time from refrigerator, and using 1 cup of the sugar, sprinkle some sugar on flat surface.
8. Roll into 2 oblong shapes, 16 x 8-inches.
9. Sprinkle some of the sugar over each oblong piece.
10. Fold both ends to center, allowing one end to overlap the other.
11. Sprinkle again with sugar and roll out to same size.

12. Repeat process a third time.
13. The last time, roll out about ¼-inch thick.
14. Cut strips 1 x 3-inches long.
15. Twist ends in opposite directions, stretching gently as you twist. Pinch ends.
16. Preheat oven to 375 degrees F.
17. Place in horseshoe shape on ungreased baking sheet, pressing down on inside edges of ends, to maintain the horseshoe shape.
18. If dough seems soft, place pan of twists in refrigerator for 30 minutes before baking.
19. Bake 8 to 10 minutes, or until light brown.
20. Remove from oven; immediately lift from baking sheet onto wire rack to cool.
21. Repeat process with other half of dough, or, if desired, dough may be refrigerated in tightly covered bowl up to 1 week.

Date Balls

My mom always enjoyed making these tasty date treats, and, of course, we all loved eating them.

Ingredients:

    1   lb. dates, finely chopped
    1   c. sugar
    2   eggs
    3   c. rice cereal
    1½ c. nuts, finely chopped
        ground nuts, coconut, or powdered sugar

Directions:

1. In small saucepan, combine dates, sugar, and eggs.
2. Over medium-low heat, cook 10 minutes, stirring constantly; remove from heat.
3. Add cereal and nuts; mix well.
4. Cool to lukewarm; butter hands and roll into balls.
5. Roll in nuts, coconut, or powdered sugar.
6. Place on wax paper to set.

Crullers

Crullers make a popular treat. Serve them warm with your choice of granulated or powdered sugar or cinnamon.

Ingredients:

1¾ c. flour
2 tsp. baking powder
½ tsp. nutmeg
½ tsp. salt
1 egg
½ c. sugar
½ c. milk
1 Tbs. butter
granulated or powdered sugar, cinnamon
oil, for frying

Directions:

1. In large bowl, sift together flour, baking powder, nutmeg, and salt; set aside.
2. In small bowl, cream egg, sugar, and butter; stir in milk.
3. Add creamed mixture to dry ingredients; blend well. Dough will be soft, but do not add more flour as crullers may become tough; divide into 3 portions.
4. Cover and place in refrigerator to chill for 1 hour.
5. Roll out 1 portion at a time on well-floured surface to a little more than ¼-inch thickness.
6. With floured knife, cut dough in strips 5 x 1-inch.
7. Twist each strip several times and fry in preheated hot, deep oil at 380 degrees F. on a frying thermometer, until golden brown, turning once.
8. Remove from oil.
9. Drain on absorbent paper; roll at once in granulated or powdered sugar, or cinnamon.
10. Repeat until all of dough is used.

French Sugar Strips

These are a delicious melt-in-your-mouth cookie and make a wonderful Mother's day treat.

Ingredients:

½ c. butter, softened
⅓ c. sugar
1 egg
1 c. flour, sifted
1 egg yolk
1 tsp. water
½ c. pecans, finely chopped
   sugar

Directions:

1. In medium bowl, cream butter, sugar, and egg; beat until light and fluffy.
2. Gradually add flour blending well into a stiff dough.
3. Divide dough in half; cover and chill in refrigerator for 1 hour.
4. Remove from refrigerator; roll out each half on baking sheets to measure 9 x 10 inches.
5. Preheat oven to 350 degrees F.
6. In small cup, combine egg yolk with water.
7. Gently brush mixture on top of dough; sprinkle with nuts and sugar. For decorative strips use colored sugar.
8. Cut into strips 1 x 2½-inches and do not separate, they will pull apart themselves when baking.
9. Bake 10 to 20 minutes, or just until lightly browned.
10. Remove from oven and place onto wire rack to cool.

Yields: 7 dozen.

Butterballs

These are a bit like shortbread and are great for packing in a tin and giving as a gift. Why not bake some for your Mom today, whether near or far? She will be sure to enjoy these as a special treat.

Ingredients:

> 2 c. cake flour
> 1 c. powdered sugar
> ½ tsp. salt
> 1 Tbs. vanilla extract
> 1 c. butter, softened
> 5 oz. almonds, slivered or chopped, toasted

Directions:

1. Preheat oven to 325 degrees F.
2. In large mixer bowl, sift together flour, powdered sugar, and salt.
3. With electric mixer on low speed, add vanilla, almonds, and butter; mix until dough forms and becomes lighter in color.
4. Shape into balls, using a rounded teaspoonful for each; place on ungreased baking sheets.
5. Bake 15 to 18 minutes, but do not brown.
6. Roll warm cookies in powdered sugar.
7. Variations: For cherry hideaways: omit almonds, and then shape dough around red or green candied cherries.
8. For date delights: substitute 1 cup ready to use diced dates for toasted almonds.
9. For chocolate nut toppers: chop almonds fine; do not add to dough. Dip top or ends of cooled cookies into ½ cup of melted semi-sweet chocolate or peanut butter pieces, then into chopped nuts.

Jam Thumbprints

These were one of my favorite cookies when I was a child. They offer a good way to use up leftover jams and jelly from your refrigerator, and the children can pick their favorites.

Ingredients:

1⅓ c. butter
⅔   c. sugar
4   egg yolks
4   egg whites, lightly beaten
2   tsp. vanilla extract
3   c. flour
½   tsp. salt
2   c. nuts, finely chopped
    jam of any flavor

Directions:

1. Preheat oven to 350 degrees F.
2. In large bowl, cream together butter and sugar until fluffy.
3. Add egg yolks and vanilla, blending well.
4. In medium bowl, mix flour with salt.
5. Gradually add to creamed mixture; mix dough until it forms a ball.
6. Shape into ¾-inch balls.
7. Dip into egg whites; roll in nuts.
8. Place on baking sheet 2 inches apart.
9. Press down the center of each cookie with your thumb.
10. Fill centers with your favorite jam.
11. Bake 10 minutes.
12. Remove from oven.
13. Place immediately on wire rack to cool.

Gingersnaps

These make a delicious treat and are great to dunk in cold milk or hot tea.

Ingredients:

3   c. flour
1   tsp. baking powder
½   tsp. baking soda
1   tsp. salt
2½ tsp. ground ginger
1   tsp. cinnamon
¼   tsp. cloves
¼   tsp. nutmeg
⅔   c. butter
½   c. sugar
¼   c. molasses
½   c. corn syrup
1   egg, well beaten
½   tsp. vanilla extract

Directions:

1. In medium bowl, sift together flour, baking powder, baking soda, salt, and spices; set aside.
2. In large bowl, cream butter and sugar; add molasses and corn syrup.
3. Blend in vanilla and egg; beat well.
4. Add flour mixture to creamed mixture, a fourth at a time, mixing well after each addition until stiff dough is made.
5. Cover and chill dough overnight or at least 6 to 8 hours.
6. Preheat oven to 350 degrees F.
7. Lightly grease baking sheets.
8. Remove from refrigerator; roll dough into small balls with floured hands.
9. Place on prepared baking sheets, 2 inches apart; flatten each ball with hand.
10. Bake 10 minutes, or until firm on top.

11. Remove from oven.
12. Immediately lift to wire rack to cool.

Molasses Crinkles

My mother used to make these when I was growing up, and I loved them. If you enjoy the taste of molasses and ginger, try these. They are delicious with a glass of ice cold milk.

Ingredients:

    3   c. butter
    4   eggs
    3¾ c. brown sugar
    1½ c. dark molasses
    ½   tsp. salt
    9½ c. flour
    4   tsp. cinnamon
    4   tsp. ginger
    2   tsp. baking soda
    2   tsp. cloves

Directions:

1. In a very large bowl, cream together butter, eggs, sugar, and molasses; set aside.
2. In another very large bowl, sift together flour, salt, and spices; add to creamed mixture and mix well into a stiff dough.
3. Cover and place in refrigerator to chill for 1 hour.
4. Preheat oven to 375 degrees F.
5. Remove from refrigerator, shape into balls, and place on baking sheet 2 inches apart.
6. Press each ball with fork to flatten.
7. Sprinkle sugar on top.
8. Bake 7 to 8 minutes, or until firm to touch.
9. Remove from oven.
10. Immediately lift to wire racks to cool.

Old-Fashioned Oatmeal Cookies

My mother used to make these old-fashioned, soft, and moist oatmeal cookies for me, and my family likes them as well.

Ingredients:

1 c. raisins
1 c. water
¾ c. butter
¾ c. sugar
¾ c. brown sugar
2 eggs
1 tsp. vanilla extract
2½ c. flour
½ tsp. baking powder
1 tsp. baking soda
½ tsp. salt
1 tsp. cinnamon
½ tsp. cloves
2 c. rolled oats
1 c. nuts, chopped

Directions:

1. Preheat oven to 400 degrees F.
2. In small saucepan, simmer water and raisins over low heat until raisins are soft and plump, 10 to 15 minutes.
3. Drain raisin liquid into measuring cup.
4. Add water to make ½ cup; set aside.
5. In medium bowl, cream butter, sugar, eggs, and vanilla.
6. In large bowl, sift together flour, baking powder, baking soda, salt, and spices,
7. Stir into creamed mixture; add oats and mix well.
8. Add nuts and raisins with the ½ cup of liquid; mix just enough to blend in.

9. Drop by rounded teaspoonfuls 2 inches apart on ungreased baking sheet.
10. Bake 10 to 12 minutes, or until lightly browned.
11. Remove from oven.
12. Place on wire rack to cool.

Russian Tea Cakes

My family loves these tasty cookies. Some people grind the nuts, but we prefer to taste and see chunks of nuts in the dough for more flavor.

Ingredients:

2	c. butter, softened
1	c. powdered sugar, divided
2	tsp. vanilla extract
4½	c. flour
1¼	c. walnuts or pecans, chopped
½	tsp. salt
	powdered sugar

Directions:

1. Preheat oven to 400 degrees F.
2. In large bowl, mix together butter, ½ cup powdered sugar, and vanilla.
3. Stir in flour, nuts, and salt until dough holds together.
4. Shape dough into 1-inch balls.
5. Place balls 1 inch apart on ungreased baking sheet.
6. Bake 10 to 12 minutes, or until set but not browned.
7. Immediately remove to wire rack; cool 5 minutes.
8. Roll warm cookies in powdered sugar; cool on wire rack 5 minutes.
9. Roll in powdered sugar again.

Peanut Butter Cookies

Our entire family loves peanut butter cookies, so we make a lot of them.

Ingredients:

½ c. butter, softened
½ c. sugar
½ c. brown sugar, firmly packed
¾ c. peanut butter
2 eggs
½ tsp. vanilla extract
1¼ c. flour
½ tsp. baking soda
½ tsp. baking powder
  additional sugar

Directions:

1. In large mixing bowl, cream butter and sugars.
2. Add peanut butter, eggs, and vanilla; beat until smooth.
3. In medium bowl, combine flour, baking soda, and baking powder.
4. Add to creamed mixture and mix well.
5. Chill dough for 1 hour.
6. Preheat oven to 375 degrees F.
7. Shape into 1-inch balls; place 2 inches apart on ungreased baking sheets.
8. Flatten each ball by crisscrossing with the tines of a fork dipped in sugar.
9. Bake 10 to 12 minutes, or until bottoms are lightly browned and cookies are set.
10. Remove from oven.
11. Place on wire rack to cool.

Yields: 4 dozen.

Snickerdoodles

Our children enjoy snickerdoodles, and this version has the addition of rolled oats that makes it even more wonderful.

Ingredients:

1	c. butter
¾	c. brown sugar
¾	c. sugar
2	eggs
1	tsp. vanilla extract
1¾	c. flour
3	tsp. cinnamon
½	tsp. salt
2	c. rolled oats
2	tsp. sugar
1	tsp. cinnamon

Directions:

1. Preheat oven to 375 degrees F.
2. Lightly grease 1 or 2 baking sheets.
3. In large bowl, cream butter, brown sugar, and ¾ cup sugar until light and fluffy.
4. In small bowl, beat together eggs and vanilla.
5. Stir into butter mixture.
6. In medium bowl, whisk together flour, 2 teaspoons cinnamon, baking soda, and salt.
7. Blend flour mixture into butter mixture; stir in oats.
8. Drop by spoonfuls onto prepared baking sheet(s), 2 inches apart.
9. In small bowl, mix together 2 teaspoons sugar and 1 teaspoon cinnamon, sprinkle over each cookie.
10. Bake 7 to 10 minutes.
11. Remove from oven.
12. Cool 2 minutes on baking sheet(s); remove to wire racks to finish cooling.
13. Store in airtight containers or freeze.

Sugar Cookies with Frosting

These are delicious sugar cookies with a creamy, buttery frosting that the whole family will enjoy.

Ingredients for cookies:

1½ c. powdered sugar
1   c. butter, softened
1   egg
1   tsp. vanilla extract
½   tsp. almond extract
3   c. flour
1   tsp. baking soda
1   tsp. cream of tartar

Ingredients for frosting:

¼   c. butter, softened
1   c. powdered sugar
½   tsp. vanilla extract
1-2 Tbs. milk, just enough for correct consistency
    few drops of food coloring

Directions for cookies:

1. Preheat oven to 375 degrees F.
2. In large bowl, cream powdered sugar and butter; add egg and extracts; mix well.
3. In medium bowl, sift together flour, baking soda, and cream of tartar; blend into creamed mixture.
4. Roll dough out to desired thickness.
5. Using any shaped cookie cutter or top of a jar lid, cut out into shapes.
6. Place 1 inch apart on a baking sheet.
7. Bake 8 minutes, or just until edges turn light brown.
8. Remove from oven.
9. Place on wire rack to cool.

Directions for frosting:

1. In small bowl, combine butter, sugar, and vanilla.
2. Add milk, a little at a time, mixing well until proper consistency for spreading without running.
3. Add food coloring if desired; spread frosting onto cooled cookies; place on wire rack for frosting to set before storing.

Mexican Wedding Cookies

Our family enjoys this type of cookie with lots of pecans mixed in to provide the extra flavor and texture.

Ingredients:

2   c. butter, softened
1   c. powdered sugar
½   tsp. salt
4   tsp. vanilla extract
4   c. flour
4½ c. pecans, finely chopped
      powdered sugar, for rolling

Directions:

1. Preheat oven to 325 degrees F.
2. In large bowl, cream butter, powdered sugar, salt, and vanilla together.
3. Blend in flour and pecans until dough holds together.
4. Shape into crescents or 1-inch balls.
5. Place 1 inch apart on an ungreased baking sheet.
6. Bake 15 to 20 minutes, or until set but not brown.
7. Remove from oven; cool slightly, then roll in powdered sugar.
8. Cool completely and roll again in powdered sugar.

English Shortbread

This makes a delicious snack to serve with your morning or afternoon tea break.

Ingredients:

2 c. butter, softened
1 c. fine sugar
3 c. flour
1 c. cornstarch
1 tsp. salt

Directions:

1. In large bowl, cream butter and sugar until blended.
2. In another bowl, mix flour and cornstarch.
3. Gradually add to butter mixture, mixing well after each addition.
4. Turn out onto lightly floured surface and knead until smooth.
5. Pat, roll, or press into 10½ x 15½-inch baking pan until smooth.
6. Score into 2-inch squares, and prick with fork.
7. Chill thoroughly; cut into squares.
8. Preheat oven to 275 degrees F.
9. Place squares on baking sheet.
10. Bake 30 minutes, or until light brown.
11. Remove from oven; lift onto wire rack to cool.
12. Place in airtight container to store.

Did You Know? . . . .

Did you know that the trend of celebrating mother's day can be attributed to the ancient Greeks? They celebrated this holiday in the spring season to honor Rhea, the mother of the gods.

Mother's Day Delights Cookbook
A Collection of Mother's Day Recipes
Cookbook Delights Holiday Series-Book 5

Desserts

Table of Contents

Page

Chocolate Boston Cream Pie

This dessert is very rich and chocolaty; it's meant for those who have a sweet tooth for chocolate.

Ingredients for cake:

1	c. flour
1	c. sugar
⅓	c. powdered cocoa
½	tsp. baking soda
6	Tbs. butter
1	c. milk
1	egg
1	tsp. vanilla extract

Ingredients for filling:

½	c. sugar
¼	c. baking cocoa
2	Tbs. cornstarch
1½	c. light cream
1	Tbs. butter
1	tsp. vanilla extract

Ingredients for glaze:

2	Tbs. water
1	Tbs. butter
1	Tbs. corn syrup
2	Tbs. baking cocoa
¾	c. powdered sugar
½	tsp. vanilla extract

Directions for cake:

1. Preheat oven to 350 degrees F.
2. Grease and flour a 9-inch round baking pan.

3. In large bowl, sift together flour, sugar, cocoa, and baking soda.
4. Add butter, milk, egg, and vanilla.
5. Beat on low speed of mixer until all ingredients are moistened; increase to medium speed for 2 minutes.
6. Pour batter into prepared pan.
7. Bake 30 to 35 minutes, or until inserted toothpick comes out clean.
8. Cool 10 minutes; turn out of pan onto wire rack.
9. Cool completely.

Directions for filling:

1. In medium saucepan, combine sugar, cocoa, and cornstarch; gradually stir in cream.
2. Cook over medium heat, stirring constantly, until mixture thickens and begins to boil.
3. Boil 1 minute, stirring constantly; remove from heat.
4. Stir in butter and vanilla.
5. Press plastic wrap directly onto surface; cool completely.
6. Cut cake into two thin layers with a piece of dental floss pulled through the cake horizontally from one side to the other.
7. Place one layer on serving plate; spread above filling over layer; top with remaining layer.

Directions for glaze:

1. In small saucepan, heat water, butter, and corn syrup to boiling.
2. Remove from heat; immediately stir in cocoa.
3. With whisk, gradually beat in powdered sugar and vanilla until smooth; cool slightly.
4. Drizzle or spread over top of cake allowing some to drizzle down sides.
5. Refrigerate until serving time.
6. Cover and refrigerate leftover cake.

Pineapple Icebox Dessert

My mom always made this for us when I was growing up. It is a great dessert to make ahead of time and freeze for a quick spare, so make two while you are at it.

Ingredients:

2   eggs
½   c. butter
3   c. powdered sugar
1   box vanilla wafers, crushed
1   lg. can pineapple, crushed, well drained (30 oz.)
1⅓ c. walnuts, coarsely ground
½   c. cream, whipped, sweetened

Directions:

1. In small bowl, cream butter, eggs, and sugar.
2. Place half of the crushed wafers in bottom of 8 x 12-inch pan.
3. Separately layer creamed mixture, half the nuts, pineapple, and whipped cream into the pan.
4. Top with remaining crumbs and nuts.
5. Refrigerate overnight, or freeze and let it thaw shortly before serving.
6. If desired, add a few chopped maraschino cherries in with pineapple for color.

Cheesecake

This is an easy-to-make version of cheesecake that is very tasty.

Ingredients:

2   pkg. cream cheese, softened (8 oz. ea.)
¾   c. sugar
¼   tsp. vanilla extract
2   eggs

1   graham cracker crust (see page 215)
1½ c. berries or fruit of choice, chopped
      extra sugar or honey

Directions:

1. Preheat oven to 350 degrees F.
2. In small bowl, mix cream cheese, sugar, and vanilla until smooth and creamy.
3. Add eggs and mix well.
4. Pour into pie crust.
5. Spoon ½ cup fruit on top; gently swirl with knife.
6. Bake 40 minutes, or until center is set.
7. Cool to room temperature then refrigerate.
8. Serve topped with remaining fruit sweetened with sugar or honey.

Creamed Berries with Wine

This is a delicious light dessert that complements a large meal.

Ingredients:

¼   c. plum wine (or other sweet, fruity wine)
2   Tbs. sugar
12 oz. fresh berries of your choice
1¼ c. whipped cream, sweetened
2   Tbs. sour cream
1   tsp. vanilla extract

Directions:

1. In medium bowl, combine berries, wine, and sugar; toss well.
2. Cover; place in refrigerator and chill.
3. When ready to serve, fold sour cream and vanilla into whipped cream.
4. Spoon creamed mixture into shallow dessert bowls.
5. Place equal amounts of berries in middle of each.

Tiramisu

Tiramisu is one of our family dessert recipes. Try this delicious recipe and enjoy.

Ingredients:

1 pkg. cream cheese, softened (8 oz.)
½ c. powdered sugar
2 Tbs. light rum or ½ tsp. rum extract
1 c. heavy whipping cream
1 pkg. French style ladyfingers (3 oz.)
½ c. cold espresso or strong coffee
2 tsp. baking cocoa

Directions:

1. In large bowl, with electric mixer on medium speed, beat cream cheese and sugar until smooth.
2. In small, chilled bowl, beat whipping cream on high speed until stiff peaks form.
3. Fold into cream cheese mixture.
4. Split ladyfingers horizontally in half.
5. Arrange half of the ladyfingers, cut sides up, on bottom of ungreased 9-inch round baking pan.
6. Drizzle half the espresso combined with the rum, over ladyfingers.
7. Spread half the cream cheese mixture over ladyfingers.
8. Arrange remaining ladyfingers, cut sides up, on top of cream cheese mixture.
9. Drizzle with remaining espresso mixture.
10. Spread with remaining cream cheese mixture.
11. Sift or sprinkle cocoa over top.
12. Cover and refrigerate 4 hours, or until filling is firm.
13. Store covered in refrigerator until ready to serve.
14. Cover and store any remaining cake.

Flan

This version of flan comes from my cousin Lynette and her husband Fred who came to visit us on the Island of St. Croix when we were first married, and we have enjoyed it ever since. Serve with a topping of your choice if desired.

Ingredients:

    6 eggs
    1 tsp. vanilla extract
    3 c. evaporated milk
    ¼ tsp. salt
    1 c. sugar
    1 Tbs. water
       topping of your choice

Directions:

1. Preheat oven to 350 degrees F.
2. In medium bowl, beat eggs well.
3. Add vanilla, milk, and salt; blend well and set aside.
4. In a 2½-quart ovenproof glass dish, combine 1 tablespoon water with 1 cup sugar.
5. Stir over medium heat.
6. Boil until sugar dissolves and becomes light brown in color.
7. Remove from heat.
8. Quickly pour the egg mixture over the sugar.
9. Place the dish in center of a baking pan half filled with water.
10. Bake 1 hour, or until it tests firm with sharp knife inserted into the middle.
11. Cool completely.
12. Place serving dish over flan and invert, so that flan comes out gently onto plate.
13. Refrigerate; chill until ready to serve.
14. Serve with a topping of your choice if desired.

Jellyroll

This delicious jellyroll can be made with a wide variety of filling.

Ingredients:

½ c. flour
1 tsp. baking powder
¼ tsp. salt
4 eggs, separated
½ tsp. vanilla extract
⅔ c. sugar, divided
½ c. jelly, jam, or other filling
   powdered sugar, sifted

Directions:

1. Preheat oven to 375 degrees F.
2. Lightly grease a 15 x 10 x 1-inch jellyroll pan.
3. In small bowl, sift together flour, baking powder, and salt.
4. In large bowl, with electric mixer on medium speed, beat egg whites until soft peaks form.
5. In small bowl, with mixer on high speed, beat egg yolks and vanilla for 5 minutes until thick and lemon colored.
6. Gradually add remaining sugar, beating until sugar dissolves.
7. Gently fold yolk mixture into whites.
8. Sprinkle flour mixture over egg mixture; fold in gently, just until combined.
9. Spread batter evenly into prepared pan.
10. Bake 12 to 15 minutes, or until cake springs back when touched.
11. Immediately loosen edges of cake from pan and turn out onto a towel sprinkled with sifted powdered sugar.
12. Starting with narrow end, roll warm cake and towel together (towel keeps cake from sticking to itself).
13. Cool on a wire rack.

14. Unroll cake and spread it with jelly, jam, or other filling to within 1-inch of edges.
15. Roll up cake without the towel and refrigerate or freeze until ready to serve.
16. Suggestions for filling: pudding or custard, pie filling, whipped cream (plain or blended with fruit), softened ice cream or frozen yogurt.

Custard

This is a simple, nutritious dessert that will have your family coming back for more.

Ingredients:

3 c. milk
3 eggs
½ c. sugar
¼ tsp. salt
½ tsp. vanilla extract

Directions:

1. Preheat oven to 375 degrees F.
2. Lightly butter a 1½-quart baking dish or 6 custard cups.
3. In medium saucepan, over medium heat, add milk and heat until small bubbles rise to surface.
4. Remove from heat.
5. In large bowl, beat eggs lightly with a fork.
6. Add sugar, salt, and vanilla; blend well.
7. Pour mixture into prepared dish or cups.
8. Place dish or cups into large baking pan half filled with hot water.
9. Bake 20 to 25 minutes for cups, 30 to 35 minutes for baking dish. Custard is done when knife inserted in center comes out clean.
10. Remove from oven.
11. Cool to lukewarm before serving.

S'more Berry Decadence

This is a delicious recipe that uses some of the tasty ingredients of S'mores and adds the delicious taste of berries for a delightful dessert. Enjoy this easy-to-make dessert.

Ingredients:

9	graham crackers, crushed
¼	c. brown sugar
⅓	c. butter
¾	c. miniature marshmallows
1	qt. vanilla ice cream or frozen yogurt
2	c. fresh berries, sliced if large
1¼	c. chocolate fudge topping

Directions:

1. Preheat oven to 350 degrees F.
2. In medium bowl, combine crackers, sugar, and butter.
3. Press firmly into bottoms of 12 muffin cups.
4. Bake 5 to 6 minutes, or until lightly brown.
5. Remove from oven and place on wire rack to cool completely.
6. Remove 6 of the bottoms and place marshmallows on the top of 6 remaining in tin.
7. Place back in oven on top rack under broiler just long enough to lightly brown; remove to wire rack to cool. These can be made ahead and stored in air-tight containers.
8. When ready to serve, place plain bottoms onto individual serving dishes; place large scoop of ice cream on top.
9. Spoon berries over ice cream, top with a marshmallow covered cracker.
10. Drizzle fudge syrup liberally over the top.

Chocolate Mousse

This makes a delicious, rich mousse for those special occasions.

Ingredients:

    1 c. semi-sweet chocolate chips
    ½ c. sugar
    ½ c. water
    5 egg yolks, beaten
    5 egg whites
    1 Tbs. unflavored gelatin
    1 Tbs. rum flavoring
    ½ tsp. cream of tartar
    ½ tsp. salt
    2 c. sweetened whipping cream, whipped
        extra whipped cream, for garnish

Directions:

1. In large bowl, over very low heat, melt chocolate stirring until smooth; cool.
2. In small saucepan, mix sugar and water together.
3. Boil 3 to 5 minutes, or until transparent and syrupy.
4. Cool slightly; slowly pour syrup in a very thin stream into beaten egg yolks, blending well.
5. Gradually stir egg mixture into melted chocolate with a whisk, and then cool.
6. In small bowl, whip egg whites with cream of tartar and salt until very stiff and glossy.
7. Fold into chocolate mixture along with whipped cream.
8. Spoon into a 2-quart soufflé dish or 2-inch mini pie crusts.
9. Refrigerate at least 4 hours.
10. Serve with a dollop of whipped cream.

Baklava

Here is a very rich, sweet dessert that will be enjoyed by many. Working with phyllo becomes fairly easy once you learn how to make this delicious recipe.

Ingredients:

> 5 c. walnuts or pecans, finely chopped
> ½ c. sugar
> 1 tsp. ground cinnamon
> 24 phyllo sheets
> 1 c. butter, melted
> 1 c. honey

Directions:

1. Preheat oven to 300 degrees F.
2. Lightly grease a 9 x 13-inch baking pan.
3. In large bowl, mix nuts, sugar, and cinnamon; portion for 6 fillings and set aside.
4. In prepared pan, place 1 sheet of phyllo, allowing it to extend up sides of pan.
5. Brush with butter; leave phyllo hanging over until top layer is added.
6. Repeat to make 3 more layers; sprinkle with nut mixture.
7. Cut 14 phyllo sheets into 7 x 11-inch rectangles to use between layers.
8. Butter between each of the 3 sheets for layers and place on top after each addition of filling, making 6 layers total.
9. Place the remaining 4 sheets, after buttering between each, on top of last filling layer.
10. Trim phyllo; pinch edges.
11. With sharp knife, cut just halfway through all the layers, in a diamond pattern to make 24 servings.

12. Bake 1¼ hours, or until top is golden brown.
13. Meanwhile, in 1-quart saucepan, over medium heat, warm honey until hot, not boiling.
14. Remove from oven.
15. Spoon honey over baklava.
16. Cool in pan on wire rack for 1 hour.
17. Cover and leave at room temperature until serving time.

Rice Pudding Custard

Rice pudding is known as a comfort food, and this is a delightful dessert that will give the meal a nice finish and leave your guests feeling very satisfied.

Ingredients:

¾ c. short-grain rice
4 c. milk
2 eggs, beaten
½ c. sugar
½ c. heavy cream
1 tsp. vanilla extract
    dash of nutmeg

Directions:

1. Preheat oven to 325 degrees F.
2. Butter an ovenproof baking dish.
3. In top of double boiler combine rice and milk; cook just until rice starts to soften.
4. Stir in beaten eggs, sugar, and nutmeg.
5. Pour the pudding into prepared dish.
6. Bake 30 minutes.
7. In small bowl, whip cream and vanilla to soft peaks.
8. Top with whipped cream.
9. Serve immediately.

Nectarine Tart

Nectarines are a nice change from peaches and make a delectable dessert for any occasion.

Ingredients:

3 lb. fresh nectarines, yellow or white, sliced
½ c. sugar
6 Tbs. instant tapioca
½ tsp. lemon peel, grated, divided
¼ c. Muscat wine or orange liqueur
1½ c. flour
½ tsp. baking powder
¼ c. sugar
10 Tbs. butter, cut into pieces
¼ tsp. lemon peel, grated
1 lg. egg

Directions:

1. Preheat oven to 350 degrees F.
2. In large bowl, combine nectarines, ½ cup sugar, tapioca, ¼ teaspoon lemon peel, and wine or liqueur; set aside.
3. In another bowl, combine flour, baking powder, and ¼ c. sugar.
4. Cut in butter thoroughly.
5. Stir in remaining lemon peel and egg to make stiff dough.
6. Press dough evenly into bottom and sides of a 9-inch springform pan.
7. Spoon in nectarine mixture.
8. Bake 1½ hours, pushing down the bubbly bits once or twice as it bakes.
9. Allow to cool 4 hours; take off springform rim.
10. Serve topped with whipped cream.

Mother's Day Delights Cookbook
A Collection of Mother's Day Recipes
Cookbook Delights Holiday Series-Book 5

Dressings, Sauces, and Condiments

Table of Contents

Page

Marinara Sauce

This is a delicious red tomato sauce that gets better as it ages. If you have the time, make it a couple days in advance and refrigerate until time to serve.

Ingredients:

 1 Tbs. safflower oil
 1 Tbs. olive oil
 1 Tbs. butter
 1 sm. onion, chopped
 2 garlic cloves, minced
 ¾ lb. mushrooms, sliced
 1 med. carrot, grated
 1 stalk celery, finely chopped
 2 Tbs. green pepper, finely chopped
 2 Tbs. fresh parsley, chopped
 1 bay leaf
 1 tsp. dried oregano
 ½ tsp. dried thyme
 ½ tsp. dried basil
 ¼ tsp. black pepper
 3 c. tomatoes, cut into quarters (28 oz. can)
 ⅔ c. tomato paste (6 oz. can)
   cayenne pepper, to taste

Directions:

1. In large saucepan heat oils and butter.
2. Stir in onion, garlic, and mushrooms; sauté until softened.
3. Add carrot, celery, green pepper, parsley, bay leaf, oregano, thyme, basil, and pepper.
4. Add cayenne pepper, to taste; mix well.
5. Cover, reduce heat, and simmer for 30 minutes.
6. Remove bay leaf.
7. Note: This sauce becomes tastier with time.

Nectarine Chutney

This is an unusually tasty chutney that enhances the flavors of roasted meats like pork or lamb. It may also be served as an appetizer with cream cheese and baked shredded chicken.

Ingredients:

2½ c. light brown sugar, packed
½ c. cider vinegar
¼ tsp. cayenne pepper
¼ tsp. ground allspice
1 lb. nectarines
2 lemons, quartered, seeded
2 med. onions
½ red bell pepper
¼ c. crystallized ginger
¾ c. golden raisins

Directions:

1. In large saucepan, place brown sugar, vinegar, cayenne, and allspice; bring to boil.
2. Reduce heat; simmer 10 minutes.
3. Pit and coarsely chop the nectarines in blender or food processor; transfer to large bowl.
4. Individually place lemons, onions, and red bell pepper in blender or food processor; process each one; add to bowl of nectarines.
5. Add raisins to nectarine mixture; toss all ingredients to blend well.
6. Add mixture to sugar mixture.
7. Continue to simmer, 30 minutes, stirring occasionally until sauce is thick.
8. Store in clean jars in the refrigerator for up to several months.

Black Raspberry Salad Dressing

This is an easy-to-make and refreshing salad dressing. My daughter Marissa likes balsamic vinegar, so she makes this often.

Ingredients:

½ c. olive oil
¼ c. balsamic vinegar
1 Tbs. black raspberry preserves
   hot sauce, to taste

Directions:

1. In a covered shaker, whisk oil and vinegar until well blended.
2. Add raspberry preserves and hot sauce to taste; blend well.
3. When ready to serve salad, drizzle over the top and enjoy the wonderful flavor.

Argentine Marinade

You will enjoy the flavors of foods that this marinade brings about. Wonderful with poultry or shellfish, this marinade can even be brushed on top of garlic bread before toasting.

Ingredients:

½ tsp. saffron threads
1 Tbs. lemon juice
½ c. virgin olive oil
½ c. white wine vinegar
1 Spanish onion, diced
2 garlic cloves, pressed
¼ c. parsley, chopped

1 tsp. thyme
  salt and pepper, to taste

Directions:

1. Powder threads and steep in lemon juice for 20 minutes.
2. In mixing bowl, whisk together oil and vinegar; blend well.
3. Add saffron and lemon juice mixture.
4. Stir in onion, garlic, parsley, and thyme.
5. Add salt and pepper to taste; whisk all together and store in a covered jar to blend flavors.

Creole Seasoning

This makes a tasty seasoning to add to your foods for a spicy, delicious taste. Sprinkle on fish, meats, veggies, and salads.

Ingredients for mix:

3 Tbs. paprika
2 Tbs. garlic powder
1 Tbs. salt
1 Tbs. onion powder
1 Tbs. dried oregano
1 Tbs. dried thyme
1 Tbs. cayenne pepper
1 Tbs. pepper

Directions:

1. In small bowl, combine all ingredients.
2. Place in a decorative shaker jar.
3. Use as preferred.

Caramel Sauce

This is a delicious and quite versatile sauce. Serve over ice cream, cake, pudding, or almost any dessert you can imagine.

Ingredients:

    2 c. brown sugar
    1 tsp. cornstarch
    ½ tsp. salt
    2 c. water
    1 c. heavy cream, whipped
    ½ tsp. vanilla extract

Directions:

1. In large saucepan, combine brown sugar, cornstarch, and salt; gradually stir in water.
2. Cook over medium heat, 20 minutes, stirring constantly until thick and clear.
3. Ladle into airtight container and refrigerate at this stage until ready to use.
4. At serving time whisk in whipped cream and vanilla.
5. Serve over your favorite dessert.

Poppy Seed Dressing

This is a great dressing and low in fat. Try it on your salad tonight and let your family know that you are health conscious.

Ingredients:

    ¾ c. sugar
    ½ Tbs. Dijon mustard

⅛ tsp. salt
¼ red onion, diced
⅔ c. red wine vinegar
2 c. oil
2 Tbs. poppy seeds

Directions:

1. In blender container add sugar, Dijon mustard, salt, onion, and red wine vinegar; blend well.
2. Add oil and poppy seeds; blend lightly.

Spicy Strawberry Sauce

Here is a recipe for a flavorful sauce to serve which is particularly delightful with fish, although it is quite delicious with any meat.

Ingredients:

1½ c. strawberry preserves
½ c. red wine vinegar
½ c. water
1 Tbs. soy sauce
¼ c. seafood cocktail sauce
1 garlic clove, minced
2 tsp. horseradish

Directions:

1. In small saucepan, combine preserves, vinegar, water, and soy sauce; blend well.
2. Stir in cocktail sauce, garlic, and horseradish.
3. Over low heat, simmer, stirring occasionally, until sauce reduces and thickens to serving consistency.
4. Serve immediately, or keep in airtight container in refrigerator for up to several weeks.

Curry Sauce

This is a recipe that takes a bit of time to cook, but it is well worth your efforts when you taste the delicious results.

Ingredients:

7 Tbs. canola oil or clarified butter
2 med. onions, finely chopped
8 garlic cloves, peeled, thinly sliced
1 pc. gingerroot, peeled, thinly sliced (3-inch)
2 mild green chilies, seeded, chopped
1 tsp. turmeric powder
1 tsp. ground cumin seed
1 tsp. ground coriander seed
2 Tbs. concentrated tomato paste with 8 Tbs. water
1 Tbs. passata

Directions:

1. In heavy skillet, over high heat, melt butter; add onion and stir for a few minutes.
2. Add garlic, ginger, and green chilies; stir for 30 seconds.
3. Reduce heat to low. Cook for 15 minutes, stirring often, to avoid browning or burning.
4. Add turmeric, cumin, coriander, tomato paste, and water; continue to cook very gently, a few minutes longer. Avoid scorching as the sauce will turn bitter; add small amount of additional water if sauce is too thick.
5. Remove from heat; cool slightly.
6. Place ¼ cup of cold water in a blender.
7. Add contents of the pan; blend until very smooth.
8. Place puréed mixture back into the skillet; stir in passata.
9. Over very low heat, simmer, covered, 20 to 30 minutes (the longer the better) stirring occasionally.

Add a small amount of hot water if sauce begins sticking to bottom of skillet, but the idea is to gently "fry" the sauce, which will darken in color to an orange brown.

10. When sauce becomes the consistency of good tomato ketchup, remove from heat.
11. Serve with your favorite bread.

Alfredo Sauce

My daughter loves Alfredo sauce, and it is very easy to make. Kelsey likes it mixed half and half with marinara sauce, which is also another excellent way to enjoy it.

Ingredients:

4 Tbs. butter
1 c. heavy whipping cream
1 pinch ground nutmeg
⅓ c. Parmesan cheese, grated
⅓ c. Romano cheese, grated
2 egg yolks, well beaten
  salt
  Parmesan cheese, grated

Directions:

1. In small saucepan, over medium heat, melt butter.
2. Add heavy cream, stirring constantly.
3. Stir in salt, nutmeg, and grated cheeses.
4. Stir constantly until cheeses are melted; whisk in egg yolks.
5. Reduce heat to medium-low; simmer 3 to 5 minutes.
6. Serve over your favorite dish.
7. Garnish with additional grated Parmesan cheese, if desired.

Dill Sauce

This is a wonderful sauce to serve with fish or to use with any type of seafood dish or salad.

Ingredients:

    ½ c. mayonnaise
    1 tsp. salt
    1 tsp. lemon juice
    1 tsp. onion, grated
    2 Tbs. dill, finely cut
        pinch of freshly ground black pepper
        pinch of sugar
        dash of hot sauce

Directions:

1. In small bowl, place mayonnaise, salt, lemon juice, onion, and dill, whisking together well.
2. Add pepper, sugar, and hot sauce to taste.
3. Whisk all ingredients together until well blended.
4. Chill before serving.

Avocado Wasabi Dressing

This is a deliciously creamy dressing with a touch of spice, so adjust the wasabi to your preference.

Ingredients:

    2 Tbs. hot wasabi
    1 ripe avocado, peeled, pitted, chunked
    1 Tbs. sour cream
    3 Tbs. apple cider vinegar
    ½ tsp. lemon juice
    ¼ tsp. garlic powder

1 pinch salt, to taste
1 pinch sugar, to taste
1 pinch black pepper, to taste
   sake or dry white wine

Directions:

1. In blender or food processor, purée all ingredients together well; add sake or other dry white wine to desired consistency.
2. Chill 1 hour.
3. Serve over salad of your choice.

Creamy Vinaigrette

Some people are hesitant to try a creamy version of vinaigrette, but it is really tasty.

Ingredients:

   ¼ c. rice wine vinegar
   2 Tbs. mayonnaise
   1 lg. garlic clove, minced
   ⅔ c. olive oil
      salt and pepper, to taste

Directions:

1. In 2-cup measuring cup, measure vinegar and mayonnaise.
2. With a small whisk, stir in garlic and a big pinch of salt and pepper.
3. Measure oil in another cup; slowly whisk oil into mixture; add first in droplets, then in a slow, steady stream while whisking to make emulsified vinaigrette.
4. Serve over your favorite salad.

Cherry Compote

This compote is delicious served with either roasted meat dishes or as a sauce over ice cream or cake.

Ingredients:

    1 c. red wine
    1 c. water
    1 pc. cinnamon stick (3-inch)
    1½ lb. fresh cherries, pitted
    1 pt. strawberries
    1 pt. raspberries or other red fruit
       several strips lemon and orange rind

Directions:

1. In small saucepan, over medium heat, add wine, water, lemon, and orange rinds.
2. Add cinnamon stick and bring to boil; reduce heat to low.
3. Add cherries; simmer 1 hour, or until cherries are softened; do not boil.
4. Transfer cherries to a bowl; boil liquid down to 1¼ cups, then pour back over the fruit through a strainer.
5. When cool, cover and refrigerate.
6. Stir hulled berries through close to serving time.

Apricot and Raisin Chutney

This chutney is very flavorful and a nice addition to your table for this special occasion.

Ingredients:

    4 c. dried apricots
    2 c. hot water
    1 pc. fresh ginger, very small, chopped
    5 lg. garlic cloves, chopped
    ¾ c. vinegar
    2 c. sugar

1 c. raisins
salt and cayenne pepper, to taste

Directions:

1. In large bowl, add apricots with hot water; cover
   and soak 4 hours.
2. In small bowl, crush and blend garlic and ginger
   with a little vinegar until smooth.
3. In large kettle, place apricots and water, garlic
   mixture and remaining vinegar.
4. Add sugar, and salt and pepper to taste.
5. Bring to boil; simmer gently for 45 minutes, stirring
   occasionally to prevent burning.
6. Add raisins; continue cooking until thick and begins
   to turn shiny; remove from heat.
7. Serve immediately or store in airtight jars for
   several weeks in the refrigerator.

Cheesy Strawberry Salsa

*This is an easy make-ahead salsa. Refrigerate until time
to serve.*

Ingredients:

1 pt. fresh strawberries, sliced
4 Roma tomatoes, seeded, chopped
1 jalapeno pepper, seeded, minced
2 garlic cloves, minced
1 lime, juiced
1 Tbs. olive oil
1 pkg. cream cheese, softened (8 oz.)

Directions:

1. In large bowl, combine all ingredients except cream
   cheese; toss together to mix and coat.
2. Cover; refrigerate 2 hours.
3. Place block of cream cheese in shallow salad bowl,
   and cover with salsa before serving.
4. Serve with plain tortilla chips.

Bolognese Sauce

This sauce is delicious served hot over spaghetti, noodles or just about any pasta.

Ingredients:

    1 lb. sweet Italian sausage, crumbled
    1 lb. lean hamburger, crumbled
    ⅓ c. olive oil
    ⅓ c. garlic, minced
    ⅓ c. onion, finely diced
    ⅓ c. celery, finely diced
    ⅓ c. carrot, finely diced
    ¼ c. green bell pepper, finely diced
    ¼ c. red bell pepper, finely diced
    1 qt. tomatoes, diced, puréed
    1 qt. tomato paste
    1 bay leaf
    ¼ c. fresh basil pesto
    ⅛ c. fresh oregano
       salt and pepper, to taste

Directions:

1. In large skillet, over medium heat, pour in olive oil; combine crumbled meats and brown lightly with garlic and onion.
2. Add celery, carrots, and peppers, stirring well.
3. Reduce heat to simmer; add tomato purée, tomato paste, bay leaf, basil pesto, oregano, and salt and pepper to taste; simmer 3 hours.
4. Serve over pasta of your choice and top with Parmesan cheese.

Did You Know? . . . .

Did you know that Mother Earth is also known as "Terra Firma"? That title is a Latin translation of some lines from one of the Greek poet, Homer's, greatest poems.

Mother's Day Delights Cookbook
A Collection of Mother's Day Recipes
Cookbook Delights Holiday Series-Book 5

Jams, Jellies, and Syrups

Table of Contents

Page

A Basic Guide for Canning Jams, Jellies, and Syrups

1. Wash jars in hot, soapy water inside and out with brush or soft cloth.
2. Run your finger around rim of each jar, discarding any with cracks or chips.
3. Rinse well in clean, clear, hot water, using tongs to avoid burns to hands or fingers.
4. Place upside down on clean cloth to drain well.
5. Place lids in boiling water for 2 minutes to sterilize and keep hot until placing on rim of jar.
6. Immediately prior to filling each jar, immerse in very hot water with tongs to heat jar (avoids breakage of jar with hot liquid).
7. Fill jar to within 1 inch of top of rim or to level recommended in recipe.
8. Wipe rim with clean damp cloth to remove any particles of food, and check again for any chips or cracks.
9. With tongs, place lid from hot bath directly onto rim of jar.
10. Using gloves, cloth, or holders, tighten lid firmly onto jar with ring or use single formed lid in place of ring to cover inner lid. Do not tighten down too hard as it may impede sealing.
11. Place on protected surface to cool, taking care to not disturb lid and ring. A slight indentation of lid will be apparent when sealed.
12. Leave overnight until thoroughly cooled.
13. When cooled, wipe jars with damp cloth and then label and date each.
14. Store upright on shelf in cool, dark place.

Chokecherry Jelly

Chokecherry jelly is also very refreshing and great on your favorite toast or English muffin. It is delicious on anything with which you use jelly, with its rich, distinctive flavor.

Ingredients:

    1   gal. chokecherries, washed
    4   c. water
    6½ c. sugar
    1   Tbs. lemon juice
    2   Tbs. powdered pectin
        sugar to add to juice (1¼ c. per cup of juice)

Directions:

1. In large pan, add chokecherries and water; bring to boil.
2. Simmer 25 minutes or until chokecherries are soft.
3. Strain through a sieve, pressing gently so you have some pulp mixed with the juice. The pulp gives body to the syrup.
4. Measure juice; place in preserving kettle, and stir in the lemon juice and pectin.
5. Heat to rolling boil; boil for 1 minute.
6. For each cup of prepared juice, add 1¼ cups of sugar, then mix in thoroughly and bring back to a rolling boil for 1 minute.
7. Remove from heat; skim foam.
8. Process following canning directions on page 186.

Did You Know? . . . .

Did you know that Rosa Parks was the mother of a bus boycott in Montgomery, Alabama that launched the Civil Rights Movement?

Apricot Jam

This is a lovely jam to place on your table and one that the whole family will enjoy.

Ingredients:

2   c. fresh apricots, pitted, mashed
1½ c. sugar
2   Tbs. lemon juice

Directions:

1. In large saucepan, combine apricots, sugar, and lemon juice.
2. Over medium heat, bring to a rapid boil.
3. Boil 20 to 30 minutes, until it reaches jelling point, stirring continuously.
4. Process following canning directions on page 186.

Apple and Raspberry Jelly

This combination of apples and raspberries makes a jelly that is really great on toast or English muffins.

Ingredients:

3 lb. raspberries, rinsed
3 lb. apples, washed, cut in quarters
   sugar (as per directions on next page)

Directions:

1. In large saucepan add raspberries; cover with water, and cook until soft.
2. Press and drain through jelly bag, removing seeds and pulp; reserve juice.

3. In large pot cover apples with water; cook until soft.
4. Press and drain through jelly bag to remove skins, seeds, and pulp; reserve juice.
5. In large kettle, combine raspberry and apple juice in equal proportions.
6. Add ⅔ cup sugar for each cup of combined juice; stir well.
7. Over medium heat, boil rapidly until jelly sheets from spoon.
8. Process following canning directions on page 186.

Apple and Pumpkin Butter

This unusual combination makes a tasty fruit butter with an autumn mix of fragrant apples and pumpkin. This is a delicious butter served on biscuits, bread, corn muffins, or hot cereal.

Ingredients:

2   c. pumpkin, cooked
1½ c. apples, peeled, cored, grated
1½ c. apple juice
½   c. brown sugar, firmly packed
¾   tsp. pumpkin pie spice

Directions:

1. In deep, heavy saucepan, combine pumpkin, apples, and juice.
2. Bring to boil; reduce heat to low.
3. Add brown sugar and spice, stirring well.
4. Simmer for 1½ hours, stirring occasionally.
5. When desired consistency is reached, remove from heat.
6. Process following canning directions on page 186.

Huckleberry Jam

Huckleberries always make a delicious jam to have on hand.

Ingredients:

4½ c. berries
1   bottle fruit pectin (6 oz.)
7   c. sugar
1   lemon, juiced, peel grated

Directions:

1. Wash fruit thoroughly.
2. Place in large cooking pot, and crush well.
3. Add lemon juice and grated peel.
4. Stir in sugar and mix thoroughly.
5. Place over medium heat; boil rapidly for 2 minutes.
6. Remove from heat and stir in fruit pectin.
7. Bring back to full rolling boil; remove from heat and skim.
8. Process following canning directions on page 186.

Carrot Raspberry Preserves

Carrots and raspberries in combination make interesting preserves and are loaded with vitamins.

Ingredients:

2 lb. carrots, peeled, sliced
2 lb. raspberries
2 lb. sugar
1 pkg. powdered fruit pectin (6 oz.)

Directions:

1. Place carrots in large saucepan with enough water to cover.
2. Bring to boil, cover, and cook until tender.
3. Drain, reserving ½ cup of liquid.
4. In blender, purée carrots and liquid; transfer to large pot.
5. Add raspberries, pectin, and sugar; stir until sugar is dissolved.
6. Bring to a slow boil; simmer gently for 20 minutes.
7. Remove from heat; skim foam from top.
8. Process following canning directions on page 186.

Apple Cider Jelly

This great tasting jelly is made from just one ingredient! The flavor is dependent on the quality and flavor of the apple cider. Great on toast or muffins or anything you choose.

Ingredients:

2 qt. apple cider

Directions:

1. In heavy saucepan, over medium heat, add cider and bring to boil.
2. Boil until reduced by half; reduce heat to low. Simmer until reaches jelling point of approximately 220 degrees F.
3. Remove from heat; cool.
4. Pour into glass jars and seal.
5. Store in refrigerator for up to 4 to 6 weeks.
6. Serve slightly chilled or at room temperature.

Raspberry Jalapeño Jelly

The combination of raspberries and jalapeño makes a refreshing jelly. It is great as a glaze for roasted pork, leg of lamb, or even a ham.

Ingredients:

1 c. raspberries, fresh or frozen
½ c. green bell pepper, chopped
¼ c. jalapeño pepper, chopped
3 c. sugar
¾ c. apple cider vinegar
1 bottle liquid pectin (6 oz.)
1 sprig fresh mint

Directions:

1. In large saucepan, combine raspberries, bell pepper, and jalapeño pepper with sugar and cider vinegar.
2. Over medium-high heat, bring to boil; boil rapidly for 1 minute; add mint sprig.
3. Remove from heat; let stand 5 minutes.
4. Stir in liquid pectin, and run the mixture through a strainer to remove bits of peppers, skins, and mint.
5. Process following canning directions on page 186.

Blueberry Jam

Blueberry jam is always a favorite with the family for toast, muffins, pancakes, or whatever else their imaginations can envision.

Ingredients:

4½ c. fresh blueberries
⅓ c. fresh lime juice
½ c. water
1 Tbs. lime rind, grated

1   pkg. pectin, powdered
4   c. sugar

Directions:

1. In 8-quart saucepan, combine berries, lime juice,
   water, lime rind, and pectin; blend well.
2. Over medium heat, bring to full boil, stirring
   constantly.
3. Quickly add sugar; stir constantly and bring to full
   rolling boil again.
4. Boil hard for 1 minute, stirring constantly.
5. Remove from heat and skim quickly if needed.
6. Process following canning directions on page 186.

Rhubarb and Fig Preserves

*This is a delicious combination of fruits and one that is
only found in a homemade preserve. It is very flavorful and
excellent for toasted breads or pancakes and waffles.*

Ingredients:

3½ qt. rhubarb
8   c. sugar
1   pt. figs, chopped
1   lemon, juiced, peel grated

Directions:

1. Cut rhubarb into small pieces; place in a large bowl.
2. Add sugar and let mixture stand overnight.
3. In the morning, place in large pot; boil until thick.
4. Add figs, lemon juice, and grated peel.
5. Cook rapidly until mixture is thick and clear.
6. Remove from heat.
7. Process following canning directions on page 186.

Black Raspberry Jelly

Black raspberries are excellent for jam or jelly making, and this recipe makes a delicious jelly.

Ingredients:

> 6 lb. black raspberries, washed, crushed thoroughly
> 7 c. sugar
> 1 Tbs. freshly squeezed lemon juice
> 1 bottle liquid pectin (6 oz.)

Directions:

1. Place raspberries in large pot; simmer covered for 10 minutes.
2. Place fruit in a jelly bag and extract all juice possible. If there is less than 4 cups, add sufficient water to measure 4 cups of juice.
3. Place raspberry juice, sugar, and lemon juice in a preserving kettle.
4. Over high heat, cook until it boils, stirring constantly; immediately stir in pectin.
5. Bring to full rolling boil; boil hard for 1 minute, stirring constantly.
6. Remove from heat; skim off foam.
7. Process following canning directions on page 186.

Red Hot Apple Jelly

This easy-to-make jelly is colorful and popular with cinnamon lovers, making a tasty treat on warm toast with butter.

Ingredients:

> 4   c. apple juice

1   pkg. powdered pectin
3½ c. sugar
½   c. red-hot cinnamon candies

Directions:

1. In large kettle, combine apple juice and pectin.
2. On medium-high heat, bring to boil stirring occasionally.
3. Add sugar and cinnamon candies, stirring well.
4. Return to rolling boil; boil hard 1 minute.
5. Remove from heat; skim foam if necessary.
6. Process following canning directions on page 186.

Rhubarb Strawberry Jam

This is a traditional way to make rhubarb jam, and the strawberry gelatin really does add quite a bit of flavor to the recipe.

Ingredients:

5 c. fresh rhubarb, chopped into sm. pieces
3 c. white sugar
1 pkg. strawberry flavored gelatin (3 oz.)

Directions:

1. In large bowl, stir together rhubarb and sugar; cover and let stand overnight.
2. Pour into large pot; over medium heat, bring to boil.
3. Reduce heat to low; boil, 12 minutes, stirring constantly.
4. Remove from heat and stir in dry gelatin mix.
5. Transfer to sterile jars, cover and refrigerate, OR process following canning directions on page 186.

Cherry Conserve

These conserves are delicious when served with toast and wonderful on pancakes or waffles.

Ingredients:

> 5 lb. Bing cherries, washed, stemmed, pitted
> 1 orange, seeded, thinly sliced
> 1 lemon, juiced
> 4 c. sugar
> 1 c. almonds or pecans, chopped
> 1 c. seedless raisins

Directions:

1. Place cherries and orange slices into a preserving kettle and add the lemon juice and sugar.
2. Cook, uncovered, 45 minutes, stirring frequently until thick and transparent.
3. Remove from heat; skim off foam.
4. Add nuts and raisins; cook another 10 minutes.
5. Remove from heat.
6. Process following canning directions on page 186.

Peach Refrigerator Jam

This is a jam that does not need to be packed in jars to keep. It can be stored for up to 3 weeks in the refrigerator in a covered container.

Ingredients:

> 2 c. fresh peaches, peeled, pitted, mashed
> 4 c. sugar
> 2 Tbs. lemon juice
> 2 tsp. ascorbic-citric powder, used for fresh fruit
> ¼ tsp. ground cinnamon
> 3 oz. liquid pectin

Directions:

1. In preserving kettle, combine peaches, sugar, lemon juice, citric powder, and cinnamon.
2. Place on medium-high heat, and bring to boil.
3. Stir in pectin; skim off foam with spoon.
4. Bring back to full rolling boil; remove from heat.
5. Pour into a large covered container or hot, sterilized jars; cover with airtight lids.
6. Let stand at room temperature until cool.
7. Store in refrigerator for up to 3 weeks.

Rose Petal Jelly

This is an unusual jelly, but it is just as delicious as the more common ones. Try this for a special gift for your mom or another special mom in your life.

Ingredients:

1 qt. fragrant rose petals, tightly packed (pesticide free)
3 c. water
1 pkg. powdered pectin
2 Tbs. lemon juice
4 c. sugar
   red food coloring (optional)

Directions:

1. In medium saucepan, heat petals and water to boiling; steep 20 minutes; strain and reserve petals.
2. Measure liquid, add water to make 3 cups.
3. Mix liquid with pectin, lemon juice and a few drops of red food coloring if desired.
4. In large, stainless steel pan, over high heat, bring mixture to boil; stir in sugar.
5. Bring to rolling boil; boil exactly 1 minute.
6. Remove from heat; skim, and stir in rose petals to prevent them from floating.
7. Process following canning directions on page 186.

Strawberry Syrup

This syrup makes a wonderful gift. Strawberry syrup is great served over pancakes, waffles, or your favorite crêpes.

Ingredients:

8 c. strawberries, crushed
¼ c. lemon juice
3 c. sugar
1 c. corn syrup
3 jars, sterilized (1 pint)

Directions:

1. In 6-quart pot, over medium heat, place strawberries; bring to boil, stirring occasionally.
2. Pour berries into damp jelly bag set over a bowl covered with double thickness of cheesecloth.
3. Let juice drip for 2 hours. There will be 3 to 4 cups of juice.
4. Return juice to pot; add lemon juice, sugar, and corn syrup.
5. Return to pot; over high heat, stir constantly and bring to rolling boil; boil 1 minute.
6. Process following canning directions on page 186.
7. Note: This recipe may be halved, covered, and refrigerated without processing when used within a few weeks.

Did You Know? . . . .

Did you know that Native American Indian women have long been honored with the name, "Life of the Nation" for their gift of motherhood to the tribes?

Mother's Day Delights Cookbook
A Collection of Mother's Day Recipes
Cookbook Delights Holiday Series-Book 5

Main Dishes

Table of Contents

Page

Game Hens with Marinade

Game hens that have been marinated in this raspberry marinade have an exquisite flavor, and are very moist and tender, making a delicious Mother's Day dinner.

Ingredients:

    6 Cornish game hens, split in half
    3 c. fresh or frozen raspberries
    1 c. raspberry vinegar
    ¾ c. olive oil
    2 bay leaves
    1 Tbs. dried thyme
       salt and pepper, to taste

Directions:

1. Rinse birds and completely pat dry.
2. Sprinkle with salt and pepper, to taste.
3. Divide split hens into two portions, and place in 2 large resealable bags.
4. In medium saucepan, combine raspberries and vinegar.
5. Heat to boiling, and boil for 1 minute.
6. Remove from heat.
7. Stir in oil, bay leaves, and thyme.
8. Cool to room temperature.
9. Pour marinade over hens.
10. Marinate overnight in the refrigerator, turning occasionally.
11. Remove hens from marinade.
12. Cook on a grill a few inches above hot coals, basting occasionally with the marinade, until juices run clear when the thickest part of a thigh is pierced.
13. Serve with your favorite side dishes or salad.

Cheddar Onion Strata

This make-ahead dish is easy to prepare and have ready for your Mother's day brunch. It may also be served with a green or fruit salad for a light dinner.

Ingredients:

- 1   tsp. canola oil
- 2   med. onions, chopped
- 8   slices rye bread, crusts trimmed
- 2   Tbs. Dijon mustard
- 1½ c. Cheddar cheese, shredded, divided
- 1   lg. tomato, seeded, coarsely chopped
- 1½ c. milk
- 4   eggs

Directions:

1. Preheat oven to 300 degrees F.
2. Lightly spray an 8 x 8-inch baking dish.
3. In large skillet, over medium-high heat, heat oil.
4. Add onions, cook 6 to 8 minutes, stirring frequently, until golden brown; remove from heat.
5. Spread mustard on 1 side of each bread slice.
6. Arrange 4 slices, mustard sides up, in baking dish.
7. Layer 1 cup cheese, tomato, and onions on bread.
8. Place remaining bread, mustard sides down, on onions.
9. In small bowl, beat milk and eggs until well-blended; pour evenly over bread.
10. Bake uncovered 1 hour, or until center is set and bread is golden brown.
11. Sprinkle with remaining cheese.
12. Let stand 10 minutes before cutting.

Yields: 6 servings.

Steak and Sweet Onions

This is an excellent choice for a great Mother's Day dinner, and even dad can help with the preparations for this meal, letting mom just sit back and relax.

Ingredients:

½ c. red wine vinegar
4 Tbs. honey
1 tsp. dried thyme, crushed
1 lg. sweet white onion, thinly sliced, separated
2 T-Bone steaks, cut ½-1-inch thick
1 tsp. cracked black pepper
4 Tbs. parsley, snipped

Directions:

1. In medium, nonreactive mixing bowl, stir together vinegar, honey, and thyme.
2. Add onion slices to vinegar mixture. Let stand while preparing meat, stirring occasionally.
3. Meanwhile, trim fat from meat; sprinkle both sides of steak with cracked pepper, pressing pepper onto the surface of the meat.
4. In large nonstick skillet, over medium-high heat, cook steaks for 10 minutes, turning once.
5. Remove steaks to a plate, reserving drippings in skillet.
6. Add onion mixture to drippings in skillet.
7. Over medium heat, cook 3 to 4 minutes, or until onions are just crisp-tender, stirring occasionally.
8. Return steaks and any meat juices that accumulated on the plate to the skillet.
9. Reduce heat to medium-low.
10. Cook uncovered, 3 to 4 minutes, or until steak is of desired doneness and liquid is slightly reduced, occasionally spooning cooking liquid over steaks.

11. To serve, transfer steaks to serving plates.
12. Stir snipped parsley into onion mixture.
13. Spoon onion mixture over the steaks.

Yields: 2 servings.

Caribbean Curried Steak

This is a nice change of pace to liven up your dinner menu. The meal is mildly spicy but well tempered when served with white rice.

Ingredients:

4 Tbs. canola oil
1 garlic clove, mashed
1 jalapeño pepper, seeded, chopped
2 green onions, chopped
2 med. white or yellow onions, peeled, chopped
2 lb. sirloin steak, cut into strips
1 Tbs. curry powder
1 tsp. ground ginger
2 c. coconut milk

Directions:

1. Heat oil in large skillet. Add garlic, jalapeño, green onions, and onion.
2. Cook, stirring for 2 minutes; add meat to pan.
3. Sprinkle meat with curry powder and ginger.
4. Continue cooking over medium heat, 5 minutes, stirring and turning, until meat is lightly browned.
5. Add coconut milk; reduce heat to low and cover.
6. Cook 10 to 15 minutes, or until the meat is tender.

Yields: 4 to 6 servings.

Mother's Day Roast Ham

This is a delicious, mouth-watering ham with an aroma that will make everyone in the house hungry. Be sure to baste several times during cooking to keep the ham moist and juicy.

Ingredients:

- 1 c. brown sugar, firmly packed
- 2 tsp. orange peel, grated
- 2 tsp. lemon peel, grated
- ½ tsp. ground ginger
- ½ tsp. ground cinnamon
- 1 fully cooked bone-in ham, butt or shank (6-9 lb.)
- 1 Tbs. whole cloves
- 1 can pineapple, sliced, sweetened; reserve juice
- 1 sm. jar maraschino cherries

Directions:

1. Preheat oven to 300 degrees F.
2. In small bowl, combine brown sugar, orange and lemon peels, ginger, and cinnamon.
3. Score top and sides of ham with knife in a crisscross pattern.
4. Place ham, scored side up, in 9 x 13-inch foil-lined roasting pan.
5. Pat ham with spice mixture and stud with cloves.
6. Pour pineapple juice in pan and place pineapple slices gently on top of ham.
7. Place a drained cherry inside each pineapple ring.
8. Bake 30 minutes; cover ham loosely with foil.
9. Bake 1¼ to 2 hours, basting every 30 minutes, until thermometer inserted in center of ham registers 135 degrees F.
10. To serve, cut a few slices from thin side of ham to form level cutting surface.

11. Transfer ham cut side down to a large cutting board. Holding ham steady with fork, cut horizontally along top of bone to cut off a boneless wedge of ham.
12. Place ham wedge cut side down on carving board and cut into thin slices.
13. Transfer slices to a serving platter. Turn ham thin side up and repeat.
14. Serve with cooked fruit, if desired.

Yields: 12 servings.

Baked Beef Burgundy

This is a simple to prepare dish that will free mom up from slaving over a hot stove and allow her to enjoy her special day while still serving a great meal.

Ingredients:

2 lb. chuck roast or stew beef, cubed
1 c. burgundy wine
1 can condensed onion soup
¼ c. dry bread crumbs, crushed finely
1 bay leaf
  pasta or rice, cooked

Directions:

1. Preheat oven to 350 degrees F.
2. In large, covered casserole dish thoroughly combine all ingredients.
3. Cover and bake 3 hours, or until tender and sauce has thickened.
4. Serve hot over cooked pasta or rice.

Yields: 4 servings.

Chicken Fried Steak

This is an old-fashioned comfort food dish, one that is a favorite time and time again. Serve it with mashed potatoes and gravy and hot homemade biscuits to sop up the gravy with.

Ingredients:

>1½ lb. round steak, bone removed, cut into pieces
>1⅓ c. flour
>2   lg. eggs
>⅓   c. milk
>1   med. onion, chopped
>1   c. chicken broth
>1   c. heavy cream
>2   Tbs. fresh parsley, chopped
>   salt and pepper, to taste
>   paprika, to taste
>   garlic powder, to taste
>   canola oil

Directions:

1. Pound steak pieces to ¼-inch thickness.
2. Rub both sides with salt, pepper, paprika, and garlic powder.
3. Heat oil in large skillet; oil should be ¼-inch high in skillet.
4. In small bowl, beat egg and milk.
5. In another bowl, season flour with a little more salt, pepper, paprika, and garlic powder.
6. When oil is hot, dredge steaks in flour, egg mixture, and flour mixture. Place immediately in hot oil.
7. Fry on both sides until golden brown.
8. Remove from skillet; set aside.
9. Remove most of the oil from skillet, leaving behind the bits of meat etc.

10. Heat remaining oil; add onion and cook until light golden brown.
11. Whisk in 3 tablespoons of seasoned flour.
12. Gradually whisk in chicken broth, scraping the bottom well. Add a little water if it is still too thick.
13. Bring to boil; add cream and parsley, and cook 1 minute.

Yields: 4 to 6 servings.

Filet Mignon with Mushrooms

This is a nice steak dish that is easy to prepare and enjoyed by all.

Ingredients:

    2 lb. filet mignon
    2 lb. mushroom caps
    6 Tbs. butter
    6 Tbs. olive oil
    1 garlic clove, chopped
    3 Tbs. parsley, chopped
      salt and pepper, to taste

Directions:

1. In skillet, over medium heat, heat oil and butter.
2. Add mushroom caps, and sauté 3 minutes.
3. Add garlic; cook until tender.
4. Sprinkle with parsley.
5. Season with salt and pepper to taste.
6. Serve over steak.
7. Serve with your favorite salad and French bread.

Yields: 4 servings.

Beef in Cranberry Chutney

This is a flavorful dish that goes well with brown rice and a light, green salad or lightly sautéed green vegetables.

Ingredients:

> 2   Tbs. canola oil
> 1½ lb. stew beef, trimmed of fat, cubed
> 1   lg. onion, chopped
> 1   celery stalk with leaves, chopped
> 1   garlic clove, minced
> 1¼ c. boiling water
> 2   c. fresh cranberries
> ½   c. raisins
> 1   Tbs. cider vinegar
> 1   Tbs. honey
> ¼   tsp. ground cinnamon
> ¼   tsp. ground ginger
> ¼   tsp. ground cloves
> ⅛   tsp. cayenne pepper, to taste
> ¼   c. walnuts, chopped

Directions:

1. Heat oil in large skillet; add beef, and brown on all sides.
2. Add onions and celery; sauté until golden brown.
3. Add garlic; sauté 1 minute, stirring constantly. Do not let garlic change color.
4. Stir boiling water into mixture; add remaining ingredients.
5. Cover; simmer 1 hour, or until beef is tender and liquid is reduced to ⅓ or ½ cup.
6. If pan juice gets too low during cooking, add a little hot water or, if pan juice does not reduce sufficiently, uncover skillet during last 30 minutes of cooking, and stir often.
7. Taste to correct seasonings.

Sweet and Sour Short Ribs

This dish is a real treat, not only is it delicious, but it is also another dish that lets mom enjoy more of her day to do as she pleases instead of being stuck in the kitchen. Be sure to get meaty ribs cut in the English style.

Ingredients:

- 3 lb. chuck short ribs
- ¾ c. flour
- 2 tsp. seasoning salt
- 1 tsp. pepper
- ½ c. canola oil
- 2 c. onions, sliced
- 1½ c. hot water
- 8 Tbs. dark brown sugar (heaping Tbs.)
- ⅓ c. catsup
- ¼ c. red wine vinegar
- 2 garlic cloves, minced
- 2 lg. bay leaves

Directions:

1. Preheat oven to 350 degrees F.
2. Trim excess fat from short ribs.
3. In medium bowl, combine flour, seasoning salt, and pepper.
4. Dredge short ribs in flour mixture.
5. In Dutch oven, heat oil. Brown the ribs on all sides; remove from pan.
6. Add onions and cook until golden brown.
7. Place ribs on top of cooked onions.
8. In medium bowl, combine water, brown sugar, catsup, vinegar, garlic, and bay leaves.
9. Pour over ribs and cover.
10. Bake 2 to 3 hours; remove bay leaves before serving.

Honey Walnut Chicken

This is a very simple chicken dish that goes well with buttered noodles and a green salad, topped off with a light dessert or fresh fruit.

Ingredients:

    2 lb. boneless, skinless chicken breasts
    1 c. honey
    2 c. bread crumbs, finely ground
    1 c. walnuts, finely ground
      salt and pepper, to taste

Directions:

1. In 2-quart dish, combine walnuts and bread crumbs.
2. Place honey in large, flat bowl or soup plate.
3. Roll chicken breasts in honey, then walnut mixture.
4. Season with salt and pepper; cover.
5. Place in refrigerator for 1 hour.
6. Preheat oven to 350 degrees F.
7. Lightly grease a 9 x 13-inch baking dish.
8. Bake 45 to 50 minutes.

Beef and Broccoli

This is a lighter dish that is quick to prepare, and it is even quicker if you prepare and refrigerate the meat and vegetables the evening or morning before.

Ingredients:

    ½ lb. sirloin steak strips
    1 lg. bunch fresh broccoli
    ½ c. carrot strips
    3 Tbs. canola oil
    ½ tsp. salt
    1 lg. onion, cut into strips
    2 Tbs. soy sauce, or to taste
    1 c. water
      oriental noodles, prepared to package directions

Directions:

1. Heat oil in large skillet; add beef strips and stir-fry 5 to 8 minutes, or until just done.
2. Parboil carrots for 2 minutes in boiling water; drain.
3. Add onion and carrots to skillet with beef.
4. Cook 3 to 4 minutes; remove from heat.
5. Add broccoli and 1 cup water; return to heat.
6. Cook 6 minutes longer, just until broccoli is tender.
7. Remove from heat; mix in soy sauce to taste.
8. Serve over prepared oriental noodles.

Salmon with Fruit

This is a mouth watering grilled salmon dish with sautéed fruit served over top.

Ingredients:

6 fresh salmon steaks, each 1½-inch thick
2 Tbs. butter
2 fresh limes, thinly sliced, leaving ends ½-inch thick
1 fresh apple, cored, halved, very thinly sliced
1 fresh pear, cored, halved, very thinly sliced
    freshly ground black pepper

Directions:

1. Preheat grill or prepare charcoal for grilling.
2. In large skillet, over low heat, melt butter and sprinkle with freshly ground black pepper.
3. Add lime slices including ends; turn to coat.
4. Add apple and pear slices; sauté 5 minutes, until butter is absorbed by the fruit. Fruit should be tender but not browned.
5. Place salmon steaks on the grill.
6. Remove lime ends; rub and squeeze over salmon.
7. Broil 5 inches from heat for 7 minutes, or until brown; turn; repeat on other side.
8. Carefully remove steaks.
9. Serve immediately with sautéed fruit.

Herb Roasted Chicken

This is a lovely dish to present on your holiday table, and it is one that takes very little time to prepare. It will leave mom free to enjoy some extra time while it is baking.

Ingredients:

¼ c. fresh herbs, basil, rosemary, marjoram, sage, or 4 tsp. dried mixed herbs, crushed
¼ tsp. salt
¼ tsp. pepper
1 whole chicken (3 lb.)
2 c. carrots, cut into ½-inch pieces
1 c. pearl onions, peeled
2 tsp. olive oil
1½ c. frozen peas, thawed

Directions:

1. Preheat oven to 375 degrees F.
2. To make herb rub, combine herbs, salt, and pepper.
3. Rinse chicken; pat dry with paper towels.
4. Loosen skin on chicken breast; using your fingers, carefully spread half the herb rub under the skin.
5. Skewer neck skin to back; tie legs to tail. Twist wings under back.
6. Place chicken, breast side up, on a rack in a shallow roasting pan. If desired, insert a meat thermometer into center of an inside thigh muscle.
7. Roast, uncovered, 30 minutes.
8. In medium casserole dish, combine carrots and onions; toss with remaining herb rub and olive oil.
9. Cover; place in oven alongside the chicken.
10. Roast 45 minutes, or until chicken is no longer pink and juices run clear, 180 degrees F. on meat thermometer, and vegetables are tender.
11. Note: Add peas the last 15 minutes of roasting.

Mother's Day Delights Cookbook
A Collection of Mother's Day Recipes
Cookbook Delights Holiday Series-Book 5

Pies

Table of Contents

Page

A Basic Recipe for Pie Crust

This is a very good recipe for a delicious, flaky crust.

Ingredients for single crust:

> 1½ c. sifted all-purpose flour
> ½ tsp. salt
> ½ c. shortening
> 4-5 Tbs. ice water

Ingredients for double crust:

> 2   c. sifted all-purpose flour
> 1   tsp. salt
> ⅔ c. shortening
> 5-7 Tbs. ice water

Directions for single crust:

1. In large bowl stir together flour and salt.
2. Cut in shortening with pastry blender or mix with fingertips until pieces are size of coarse crumbs.
3. Sprinkle 2 tablespoons ice water over flour mixture, tossing with fork.
4. Add just enough remaining water 1 tablespoon at a time to moisten dough, tossing so dough holds together.
5. Roll pastry into 11-inch circle, and wrap in plastic wrap; refrigerate for 1 hour.
6. Preheat oven to 425 degrees F.
7. Remove plastic wrap from pastry, and fit pastry into a 9-inch pie plate.
8. Fold edge under and then crimp between thumb and forefinger to make fluted crust.
9. For filled pie with an instant or cooked filling (cream-filled, custard-filled, etc.), prick crust all over with fork then bake 15 to 20 minutes until done.
10. If preparing pie with uncooked filling (such as pumpkin), do not prick crust; pour filling into unbaked pastry shell, and then bake as directed.

Directions for double crust:

1. Turn desired filling into pastry-lined pie plate; trim overhanging edge of pastry ½ inch from rim of plate.
2. Cut slits with knife in top crust for steam vents.
3. Place over filling; trim overhanging edge of pastry 1 inch from rim of plate.
4. Fold and roll top edge under lower edge, pressing on rim to seal; flute.
5. Cover fluted edge with 2- to 3-inch-wide strip of aluminum foil to prevent excessive browning.
6. Remove foil during last 15 minutes of baking.

Yields: 1 pie crust (9-inch single or double).

A Basic Cookie or Graham Cracker Crust

This is a great crust for use with cream pies or for an unbaked pie. Use your favorite flavor of cookie to complement your filling, or use graham crackers.

Ingredients:

2 c. cookie or graham cracker crumbs, finely crushed
⅓ c. sugar
½ c. butter, melted

Directions:

1. Combine crumbs, sugar, and butter.
2. Press mixture firmly against bottom and up sides of 9-inch pie plate.
3. Baking is not necessary, but if preferred crust may be baked at 400 degrees F. for 10 minutes.

Yields: 1 pie crust (9-inch).

Huckleberry Custard Pie

This is an excellent dessert pie that makes a delicious and attractive dessert to top off your special dinner.

Ingredients for filling:

4 eggs, slightly beaten
6 Tbs. milk
1¾ c. sugar
¼ c. flour
4 c. huckleberries

Ingredients for crust:

2¼ c. flour
1 tsp. salt
⅔ c. canola oil
4 Tbs. cold water

Directions for crust:

1. In large bowl, combine flour and salt.
2. Blend in oil with fork until mixture becomes crumbly.
3. Sprinkle water over mixture; mix until dough clings together.
4. Divide dough into two parts and shape into balls; flatten each slightly.
5. Roll one ball into a circle between two squares of wax paper until an inch wider than the pie tin.
6. Peel off top paper; place pastry into 9-inch pie pan.
7. Roll other ball out in same manner for lattice top.
8. Peel off top paper; cut into strips 1-inch wide; set aside.

Directions for filling:

1. Preheat oven to 350 degrees F.
2. In medium bowl, beat eggs and milk together.
3. Add sugar and flour, blending well.

4. Gently fold in huckleberries.
5. Pour filling into pastry-lined pie pan.
6. Divide cut strips in half; place on top of pie crust in a lattice design by placing a strip across one side, turn pie half way around and then lay another strip in opposite direction.
7. Continue turning with each strip until all are used; trim off overhang of strips and pinch together with the bottom pie crust all the way around.
8. Bake 50 minutes, or until inserted toothpick comes out clean.
9. Place on wire rack to cool before slicing to serve.

Rhubarb Custard Pie

The combination of tart rhubarb and cream custard is delicious. Try some French vanilla ice cream on the top to dress it up even more for this special occasion.

Ingredients:

1½ c. sugar
4   eggs, lightly beaten
¾   c. half and half cream
⅛   tsp. salt
4   c. rhubarb, coarsely chopped
1½ Tbs. flour
1   9-inch pie shell (see A Basic Pie Crust page 214)

Directions:

1. Preheat oven to 375 degrees F.
2. Make pastry dough.
3. In large bowl, combine sugar, eggs, half and half, and salt; beat well.
4. Add rhubarb; mix well.
5. Sprinkle flour evenly over bottom of pie crust.
6. Slowly pour filling into crust.
7. Bake on lower rack for 1 hour, or until center is set.
8. Cool on wire rack before slicing to serve.

Amish Apple Pie

My husband and I lived in Iowa City for four years and it was always a treat to go to visit the Amish colonies! They served an Amish apple pie that was so delicious we obtained a recipe and still like to bake and enjoy it at home.

Ingredients:

- 1   c. sour cream
- 1   egg
- ½   c. sugar
- 2   Tbs. flour
- ¼   tsp. salt
- 3   c. apples, diced, peeled
- 1   tsp. vanilla extract
- 1   9-inch pie shell (see A Basic Pie Crust page 214)

Ingredients for crumb topping:

- ½   c. brown sugar
- ⅓   c. flour
- ⅓   c. butter
- 1½ tsp. cinnamon

Directions:

1. Preheat oven to 400 degrees F.
2. In small bowl, combine topping ingredients; mix until crumbly.
3. In medium bowl, beat sour cream and egg together; add flour, sugar, salt, and vanilla. Mix until smooth.
4. Stir in apples.
5. Bake 25 minutes; remove pie from oven.
6. Sprinkle crumb topping over top; return pie to oven.
7. Bake 20 to 30 minutes.
8. Cool and serve.

Banana Cream Pie

My son Kyler and daughter Kelsey particularly enjoy this pie and so would your guests. This recipe has more bananas and pudding for extra flavor.

Ingredients:

- ¾ c. sugar
- ½ c. flour
- ¼ tsp. salt
- 3 c. whole milk
- 3 egg yolks, beaten
- 3 Tbs. butter
- 1¼ tsp. vanilla extract
- 1 9-inch pie crust, baked (see A Basic Pie Crust page 214)
- 5 bananas, sliced

Directions:

1. Preheat oven to 350 degrees F.
2. In small saucepan, combine sugar, flour, and salt; add milk gradually while stirring gently.
3. Cook over medium heat, stirring constantly, until the mixture is bubbly; continue cooking 2 minutes longer.
4. Stir a small quantity of the hot mixture into the beaten egg yolks, and immediately add egg yolk mixture back to the hot mixture.
5. Cook 3 more minutes, stirring constantly to avoid burning.
6. Remove from heat; add butter and vanilla; stir until a smooth consistency; cool to lukewarm.
7. Slice bananas into the cooled, baked pastry shell and pour in the filling.
8. Bake 12 to 15 minutes.
9. Chill in refrigerator for 1 hour.

Caramel Pecan Pie

This is a very easy-to-make pie with the delicious taste of caramel and pecans.

Ingredients for crust:

> 1 c. quick oats
> ½ c. pecans, chopped
> ⅓ c. brown sugar, packed
> ½ tsp. cinnamon
> ¾ c. butter, melted

Ingredients for filling:

> 1 can sweetened condensed milk (14 oz.)
> 1 c. pecans, chopped
> ½ c. brown sugar, packed
>   pinch of salt

Directions for crust:

1. Preheat oven to 375 degrees F.
2. In small bowl, combine oats, pecans, brown sugar, and cinnamon.
3. Pour in butter and blend well.
4. Press mixture into bottom and up sides of a 9-inch pie plate.
5. Bake 8 to 10 minutes.

Directions for filling:

1. In top of double boiler combine milk, sugar, and salt.
2. Cook over rapidly boiling water, 10 minutes, stirring often until thickened.
3. Remove from heat; stir in half the nuts.
4. Pour into pie shell; sprinkle with remaining nuts.
5. Cool and top with whipped cream.

Chocolate Banana Cream Pie

My mom and dad always enjoyed chocolate cream pie. My mom would make it for family and guests quite often, and now my own son Kyler and my daughter Kelsey often request this pie with the addition of bananas.

Ingredients:

- 4 lg. egg yolks
- 1½ c. sugar
- ⅓ c. cornstarch
- ½ tsp. salt
- 3 c. milk
- 2 oz. unsweetened baking chocolate
- 2 Tbs. butter, softened
- 1 Tbs. and 1 tsp. vanilla extract
- 2 lg. bananas, sliced
- 1 9-inch pie crust, baked (see A Basic Pie Crust page 214)
  toffee bits, for garnish

Directions:

1. In medium bowl, beat egg yolks with fork; set aside.
2. In 2-quart saucepan, mix sugar, cornstarch, and salt; gradually stir in milk.
3. Cook over medium heat, stirring constantly, until mixture thickens and comes to a boil; boil 1 minute.
4. Immediately stir at least half of the hot mixture gradually into egg yolks, and then stir yolk mixture back into remaining hot mixture in the saucepan.
5. Boil and stir 1 minute; remove from heat and cool to lukewarm.
6. Slice 2 large bananas into pie crust; pour warm filling over bananas.
7. Refrigerate 2 hours until set; cut into wedges.
8. Garnish each serving with a dollop of whipped cream, toffee bits, and banana slices if desired.

Coconut Cream Pie

My mom and dad used to enjoy coconut cream pie, so my mom would make it for family and guests on a frequent basis.

Ingredients:

- 4 lg. egg yolks
- ⅔ c. sugar
- ¼ c. cornstarch
- ½ tsp. salt
- 3 c. milk
- 2 Tbs. butter, softened
- 2 tsp. vanilla extract
- 1½ c. coconut, flaked, not toasted
- 1 basic pie crust, baked (see A Basic Pie Crust page 214)

Ingredients for topping:

- 1 c. sweetened whipped cream
- ½ c. coconut, toasted

Directions:

1. In medium bowl, beat egg yolks with a fork; set aside.
2. In 2-quart saucepan, mix sugar, cornstarch, and salt; gradually stir in milk.
3. Cook over medium heat, stirring constantly, until mixture thickens and boils.
4. Boil and stir 1 minute.
5. Immediately stir at least half of the hot mixture gradually into egg yolks, and then stir back into hot mixture in saucepan.
6. Boil and stir 1 minute; remove from heat.
7. Stir in butter, vanilla, and coconut.
8. Pour into baked pie crust; cover with plastic wrap to prevent hard layer from forming on top.

9. Refrigerate 2 hours, or until set.
10. Remove plastic wrap.
11. Top with sweetened whipped cream and toasted coconut.
12. Cover and refrigerate cooled pie until serving.
13. Store covered in refrigerator.

Frozen Grasshopper Pie

Step three is an important step that I sometimes try to rush, and it does not work. The marshmallow mixture must be totally cooled, or it will wilt the whipped cream and will not be as tasty as it should be. This pie is always great to have stashed away in the freezer for unexpected company or an unplanned dessert.

Ingredients:

16 chocolate sandwich cookies, crushed
2 Tbs. butter, melted
⅓ c. sugar
2⅔ c. hot milk
1⅓ c. crème de menthe
¾ c. crème de cacao
2 c. mini marshmallows
6 c. whipped cream, beaten

Directions:

1. In medium bowl, combine sandwich cookies and sugar with butter.
2. Press mixture into pie pan to form chocolate crust.
3. Melt marshmallows in hot milk; cool to lukewarm.
4. Add crème de menthe and cacao; blend well.
5. Place mixture into refrigerator until chilled; blend in whipping cream.
6. Pour filling into chocolate crust.
7. Chill until ready to serve.

Key Lime Pie

My husband and I lived in the Virgin Islands and thus traveled to the Keys. We loved the many different versions of the Key Lime Pies that we were fortunate to try.

Ingredients:

1 c. sugar
¼ c. flour
3 Tbs. cornstarch
¼ tsp. salt
2 c. water
3 eggs, separated
1 Tbs. butter
¼ c. lime juice
1 lime, zested (be careful not to use the bitter part)
¼ tsp. cream of tartar
6 Tbs. sugar
1 pie crust, baked (see A Basic Pie Crust page 214)

Directions:

1. Preheat oven to 425 degrees F.
2. In small bowl, beat egg yolks well; set aside.
3. In medium saucepan, combine sugar, flour, cornstarch, and salt; gradually stir in water.
4. Cook over medium heat until thickened, stirring to keep from scorching.
5. Gradually pour cooked sugar mixture into the beaten egg yolks, beating continually while adding.
6. Return mixture to low heat and cook, stirring constantly, for 2 minutes.
7. Stir in butter, lime juice, and lime zest; cool to lukewarm.
8. In medium bowl, beat egg whites until light and frothy; add cream of tartar and continue beating until stiff peaks form.
9. Gradually beat in sugar; beat until stiff and glossy.
10. Pour filling into prepared pie shell.

11. Pile meringue on top, spreading until it touches the edges of the pastry to prevent the meringue from shrinking.
12. Bake 5 to 6 minutes, or until meringue is golden brown.
13. Place on wire rack to cool completely.
14. Refrigerate if not using in short time.

Blueberry Cream Pie

This is a refreshing and attractive chilled blueberry pie that tastes even more delicious than it looks.

Ingredients:

3 oz. cream cheese
½ c. powdered sugar
1 tsp. vanilla extract
½ c. whipping cream
2 c. fresh blueberries
1 c. sugar
½ c. water
3 Tbs. cornstarch
1 pie crust, baked (see A Basic Pie Crust page 214) fresh blueberries, for garnish

Directions:

1. In medium bowl, combine cream cheese, powdered sugar, and vanilla.
2. Spread cream mixture onto bottom of pie shell.
3. In medium saucepan, combine blueberries, sugar, water, and cornstarch; bring to boil, stirring constantly.
4. Cook until thickened; cool to lukewarm.
5. Pour over cream mixture in pie shell; chill in refrigerator.
6. Whip the cream and spread on top of chilled pie.
7. When ready to serve, top with fresh blueberries.

Pecan Pie

Pecans are a delicious addition to any food and this pie will remind you why. It is a very rich, full-flavored pie that will please all.

Ingredients:

    3   eggs
    1   c. dark corn syrup
    1   c. sugar
    2   Tbs. butter, melted
    1   tsp. vanilla extract
    ⅛   tsp. salt
    1½ c. pecans, chopped
    1   pie shell, unbaked (see A Basic Pie Crust page 214)
         additional pecan halves

Directions:

1. Preheat oven to 400 degrees F.
2. In large bowl, beat eggs slightly.
3. Mix in corn syrup, sugar, butter, vanilla, and salt; stir in nuts.
4. Pour into unbaked pastry shell.
5. Garnish top with pecan halves.
6. Bake 15 minutes.
7. Reduce heat to 350 degrees F.
8. Bake an additional 30 to 35 minutes. Filling should be slightly less set in center than around edge.
9. Remove from oven.
10. Place on wire rack to cool.
11. Serve warm with homemade vanilla bean ice cream or sweetened vanilla flavored whipped cream.
12. Refrigerate leftovers.

Yields: 8 servings.

Mother's Day Delights Cookbook
A Collection of Mother's Day Recipes
Cookbook Delights Holiday Series-Book 5

Preserving

Table of Contents

Page

A Basic Guide for Canning, Dehydrating, and Freezing

1. Place empty jars in hot, soapy water. Wash well inside and out with brush or soft cloth.
2. Run your finger around rim of each jar, discarding any that are chipped or cracked.
3. Rinse in clean, clear, very hot water, being careful to use tongs to avoid burning skin or fingers.
4. Place upside down on towel or fabric to drain well.
5. Place lids in boiling water bath for 2 minutes to sterilize and keep hot until ready to place on jar rims.
6. Immediately prior to filling jars with hot food, immerse in hot bath for 1 minute to heat jars. Heating jars avoids breakage.
7. If filling with room-temperature food, you need not immerse immediately prior to filling.
8. Fill jars with food to within ½ inch of neck of jars.
9. When ladling liquid over food, fill jars to 1 inch from top rim in each jar. This leaves air allowance for sealing purposes.
10. Wipe rims of jars with damp, clean cloth to remove any particles of food and again check for chips or cracks.
11. Using tongs, place lids from hot bath directly onto jars.
12. Place rings over lids, and using cloth, gloves, or holders, tighten down firmly while hanging onto jars.
13. Do not tighten down too hard as air may become trapped in jars and prevent them from sealing.
14. For fruits, tomatoes, and pickled vegetables, place each jar into water bath canning kettle so water covers jars by at least 1 inch.
15. For vegetables, process them in a pressure canner according to manufacturer's directions.
16. Follow time recommended for food being canned.
17. Do not mix jars of food in same canning kettle as times may vary for each kind of food.

18. At end of time recommended for canning, gently lift each jar out of bath with tongs, and place on protected surface.
19. Turn lids gently to be sure they are firmly tight.
20. Place filled, ringed jars on cloth to cool gradually.
21. Do not disturb rings, lids, or jars until sealed.
22. Lids will show slight indentation when sealed.
23. When cool, wipe jars with damp cloth then label and date each jar.
24. Leave overnight until thoroughly cooled.
25. Jars may then be stored upright on shelves.

Dehydrating

1. Always begin with fresh, good quality food that is clean and inspected for damage.
2. Pretreatment is not necessary, but food that is blanched will keep its color and flavor better. Use the same blanching times as you would for freezing. Fruit, especially, responds to pretreatment.
3. Doing some research on pretreatments may help you decide what procedure you would like to use.
4. You can marinate, salt, sweeten, or spice foods before you dehydrate them.
5. Jerky is meat that has been marinated and/or flavored by rubbing spices into it; avoid oil or grease of any kind as it will turn rancid as the food dries.
6. Vegetables and fruit can be treated the same way.
7. Slice or dice food thin and uniform so that it will dehydrate evenly. Uneven thicknesses may cause food to spoil because it did not dry as thoroughly as other parts.
8. Space food on dehydrator tray so that air can move around each piece.
9. Try not to let any piece touch another.
10. Fill your trays with all the same type of food as different foods take different amounts of time to dry.

11. You can, of course, dry different types of food at the same time, but you will have to remember to watch and remove the food that dehydrates more quickly. You can mix different foods in the same dehydrator batch, but do not mix strong vegetables like onions and garlic as other foods will absorb their taste while they are dehydrating.

12. The smaller the pieces, the faster a food will dehydrate. Thin leaves of spinach, celery, etc., will dry fastest. Remove them from the stalks before drying them or they will be overdone, losing flavor and quality. In very warm areas, they might even scorch. If they do, they will taste just like burned food when you rehydrate them.

13. Dense food like carrots will feel very hard when they are ready. Others will be crispy. Usually, a food that is high in fructose (sugar) will be leathery when it is finished dehydrating.

14. Remember that food smells when it is in the process of drying, so outdoors or in the garage is an excellent place to dry a big batch of those onions!

15. Always test each batch to make sure it is "done."

16. You can pasteurize finished food by putting it in a slow oven (150 degrees F.) for a few minutes.

17. Let the food cool before storing.

18. Store in airtight containers to guard against moisture. Jars saved from other food work well as long as they have lids that will keep moisture out.

19. Zip-closure food storage bags work well.

20. Jars of dehydrated carrots, celery, beets, etc., may look cheerful on your countertop, but the colors and flavors will fade. Dehydrated food keeps its color and flavor best if stored in a dark, cool place.

21. Dehydrating food takes time, so do not rush it. When you are all done, you will have a dried food stash to be proud of!

Freezing

1. Wash all containers and lids in hot, soapy water using soft cloth.
2. Rinse well in clear, clean, hot water.
3. Cool and drain well.
4. Place food into container to within 1 inch of rim. This allows for expansion of food during freezing.
5. Wipe rim of container with clean damp cloth, checking for chips or breaks.
6. Be certain cover fits the container snugly to avoid leaks. Burp air from container.
7. If food is hot when placing in container, cool prior to placing in freezer.
8. Label and date each container.
9. Store upright in freezer until frozen solid.

Tomatoes

Bright red tomatoes are always nice to have on the shelf and can be used in many ways throughout the year.

Ingredients:

    1½ tsp. canning salt
    1   qt. tomatoes

Directions:

1. In large pot, drop tomatoes in boiling water for 1 minute; remove and set in colander.
2. Skins should slip off easily at this point.
3. Drop tomatoes in boiling water again; allow water to come to a boil and boil for 3 minutes.
4. Put tomatoes in jars and process following canning directions on page 228.

Dried Cherries

This is a wonderful way to preserve those delicious cherries for winter use or longer if desired.

Ingredients:

   3 lb. Northwest sweet cherries

Directions:

1. Select firm, ripe fresh sweet cherries; wash, remove stems, cut in half, and pit.
2. Place cherries, skin side down, in single layers on dehydrator trays.
3. Dry cherries at 140 degrees F. for 6 to 12 hours, being careful not to over dry. Cherries should be leathery and slightly sticky when properly dried.
4. To store, place in small plastic bags; remove air and seal.
5. Keep in dark, dry, cool place for storage.
6. Note: Dried cherries are a great substitute for raisins or dried currants in recipes and as a snack.

Kiwi Fruit Leather

This is a great way for preserving kiwis when you are able to catch a great sale, and they do not look like they will be used or eaten fast enough.

Ingredients:

   10 kiwi fruit, peeled
   2 Tbs. white grape juice concentrate
   ¼ c. sugar
   2 Tbs. lemon juice
      green food coloring, if desired

Directions:

1. In blender container add all ingredients; purée so seeds are pulverized. Spread fruit in roll trays.
2. Process following dehydrating directions on page 228.
3. Dry until leathered; wrap in wax paper.
4. Store in airtight jar, in cool, dark place, or refrigerate until ready to serve.

Sweet Pickled Onions

Try these sweet pickled onions on your next appetizer tray. Your guests or family both will enjoy the delicious crisp taste and texture.

Ingredients:

16 med. boiling onions, peeled
1½ c. malt vinegar
½ c. water
3½ Tbs. dark brown sugar, packed
2 Tbs. pickling spice
1 piece fresh ginger, peeled, sliced (1-inch)

Directions:

1. Cover onions with water in 2 to 3-quart heavy saucepan; simmer 5 minutes only as onions should be still lightly crisp.
2. Drain and transfer to clean, heatproof jar.
3. Simmer remaining ingredients in saucepan 5 minutes; pour over onions to cover.
4. Cool completely, uncovered.
5. Cover; chill in refrigerator for at least 1 week to allow flavors to develop.
6. Pickled onions can be kept 3 weeks in refrigerator.

Pickled Peaches

Pickled peaches make a nice accompaniment to a roasted ham, duck, or chicken dish.

Ingredients for peaches:

8 lb. sm., firm peaches
1 gal. water, cold
2 Tbs. pickling salt
2 Tbs. white vinegar
2 Tbs. whole cloves

Ingredients for pickling syrup:

1 qt. white vinegar
1 qt. water
3 lb. sugar
4 cinnamon sticks

Directions:

1. In large pot, combine water, salt, and vinegar.
2. In another large pot, boil enough water to dip peaches in for a few seconds.
3. Remove; dip in cold water, salt, and vinegar mixture, to slip skins. To prevent discoloration; leave whole or halve, but do not remove pits.
4. Stud each peach with 2 cloves.
5. Place syrup ingredients in a large enamel or stainless steel kettle and bring to boil.
6. Add peaches, a few at a time, and simmer, uncovered, 5 to 7 minutes until barely tender, but still crisp.
7. Remove peaches with slotted spoon; set aside.
8. Repeat with remaining peaches.
9. When all are cooked, bring syrup to boil and pour over peaches; cover and let stand overnight.
10. The next day, wash and sterilize ten 1-pint jars and their closures.

11. At same time, drain syrup from peaches, reserving syrup.
12. Discard cinnamon sticks.
13. Pour syrup into a saucepan and bring to boil.
14. Pack peaches into hot jars.
15. Pour in boiling syrup, filling to within ¼-inch of top.
16. Process following canning directions on page 228.
17. Store in a cool, dark place 4 to 6 weeks before serving.

Smoked Turkey Jerky

This is a delicious way to preserve turkey when you come upon an ample supply. It is always good for a healthy treat.

Ingredients:

½ c. soy sauce
4 Tbs. sugar
2 tsp. fresh ginger, grated
1 garlic clove, minced
1 Tbs. liquid smoke
2 lb. turkey breast or thighs, cooked, sliced paper thin

Directions:

1. In medium bowl, combine all ingredients except turkey.
2. Dip meat slices into mixture.
3. Place dipped meat in layers in a bowl or dish; pour remaining mixture over meat.
4. Cover tightly; marinate in refrigerator 6 to 12 hours; rotate layers of meat occasionally.
5. Place slices single layered in dehydrator until dry. While meat is drying, occasionally blot excess oil with paper towels.
6. Store in airtight container in refrigerator.

Spiced Crab Apples

Spiced crab apples are very delicious. Preserving them is very handy for use as garnishes.

Ingredients:

    6   lb. crab apples
    4½ c. apple vinegar (5% acidity)
    4   c. water
    7   c. sugar
    5   tsp. whole cloves
    5   sticks cinnamon
    7   cubes of fresh gingerroot

Directions:

1. Remove blossom petals, and wash apples, leaving stems attached.
2. Place all spices in spice bag or cheesecloth tied with string.
3. Puncture the skin of each apple four times with an ice pick or toothpick.
4. In large pot, combine vinegar, water, and sugar; bring to boil; add spices.
5. Using a blancher basket or sieve, immerse ⅓ of apples at a time in boiling vinegar solution for 2 minutes. Repeat with remaining apples.
6. Place cooked apples and spice bag in a clean 1 or 2-gallon crock.
7. Add hot syrup.
8. Cover and let stand overnight.
9. Remove spice bag; drain syrup into a large saucepan and reheat to boiling.
10. Process following canning directions on page 228.

Bread and Butter Pickles

*My aunt used to can lots of bread and butter pickles,
and they are great to have on your pantry shelf.*

Ingredients:

8 lb. cucumbers, thinly sliced
1 lb. onions, thinly sliced
2 gal. water
2 c. pickling lime
9 c. sugar
2 Tbs. salt
2 Tbs. celery seed
2 Tbs. pickling spice
8 c. vinegar
5 c. water

Directions:

1. In large pot, soak cucumbers and onions in a
    mixture of 2 gallons water and 2 cups pickling lime
    for 24 hours; stir a few times throughout soaking
    time.
2. Rinse well.
3. Let stand in ice water for 3 hours; drain.
4. In large processing kettle, combine sugar, salt,
    celery seed, pickling spice, vinegar, and 5 cups
    water to make syrup.
5. Add cucumbers and onions.
6. Over medium heat, cook 1½ hours.
7. With slotted spoon, pack hot jars with cucumbers
    and onions.
8. Fill jars with syrup leaving ½-inch headspace.
9. Process following canning directions on page 228.

Brandied Cherries

These brandied cherries are delicious used as a garnish on other dishes.

Ingredients:

6 c. sweet cherries, red, yellow or both
2 c. brandy
2 c. sugar
1 c. water

Directions:

1. Wash cherries and remove stems.
2. Place cherries in jars; cover totally with brandy.
3. Cover the jars, but do not seal; let stand overnight.
4. In saucepan add sugar and water; bring slowly to boil; stirring until sugar dissolves.
5. Boil 10 minutes; skim surface and cool.
6. Drain brandy from cherries; add to syrup and stir well.
7. Pour liquid back into jars to cover cherries; seal.
8. Let stand at least one month before using.

Strawberry Rhubarb Rollup

This is a healthy treat and a great way to use your spring fruits. Children particularly love to eat these rollups.

Ingredients:

1½ c. fresh strawberries, washed, hulled, sliced
½ c. fresh rhubarb, cut into 1-inch pieces
½ c. sugar

Directions:

1. In small saucepan boil rhubarb just until soft; drain.
2. In blender add strawberries and rhubarb; process until well puréed.

3. Pour into saucepan; add sugar. Over medium heat, cook 5 minutes.
4. Line baking sheet with parchment paper.
5. Spoon mixture onto paper; leave space near edges.
6. Spread as thin as possible, about ⅛-inch thick.
7. Repeat until you've used up all your fruit.
8. Turn oven temperature to 150 degrees F.; place tray on upper rack. Leave overnight with door slightly ajar to let moisture escape while drying fruit.
9. When dry, cut into rectangles; roll in plastic wrap.
10. Store in airtight containers in a dark, cool place.

Spiced Pickled Beets

This is a spicier version of pickled beets than most recipes. If you like flavor, by all means, try this recipe.

Ingredients:

4 lb. sm. beets, roots and 2-inch stems left on
2 c. sugar
2 c. water
2 c. vinegar
1 tsp. ground cloves
1 tsp. allspice
1 Tbs. cinnamon

Directions:

1. In large pot, place beets with enough water to cover.
2. Cook until tender.
3. Place in cool water; slip skins off and rinse.
4. Slice or quarter beets after peeling.
5. In large saucepan combine sugar, spices, vinegar, and water; add beets, over low heat, simmer 15 minutes.
6. Remove beets; pack into hot, sterilized jars.
7. Boil liquid again; pour into jars leaving ½-inch headspace.
8. Process following canning directions on page 228.

Blueberry Applesauce Fruit Leather

This is excellent fruit leather, and it makes a great snack that all moms would approve of.

Ingredients:

  1 c. blueberry purée
  1 c. unsweetened applesauce
  1 Tbs. honey, or to taste

Directions:

1. In blender or food processor, combine blueberries and applesauce; process until smooth.
1. Pour mixture through a strainer or sieve to remove skin and seeds.
2. Place mixture in 10-inch skillet; stir in honey to taste.
3. Over very low heat, cook 1 hour, stirring frequently, until thickened.
4. Line a baking sheet with parchment paper.
5. Preheat oven to 150 degrees F.
6. Pour thickened mixture onto parchment paper and spread to form a rectangle ⅛-inch thick.
7. Bake 5½ to 6 hours, until fruit is dry enough not to stick to your fingers but moist enough to roll. Place a potholder in oven door to keep it ajar will help dry the leather.
8. Remove from oven and cool.
9. Cut leather in 4 to 5-inch squares or rectangles on plastic wrap and roll up.
10. Store in an airtight container.

Did You Know? . . . .

Did you know that Mother Goose is one of the most popular of all children's entertainers? Her books and stories have been loved for many generations.

Mother's Day Delights Cookbook
A Collection of Mother's Day Recipes
Cookbook Delights Holiday Series-Book 5

Salads

Table of Contents

Page

Fresh Fruit Salad

This makes a very attractive and colorful salad as well as refreshing and flavorful with the poppy seed dressing. Select your favorite fresh fruits to replace those listed below and enjoy.

Ingredients for poppy seed dressing:

1¼ c. honey
1 Tbs. dry mustard
1 tsp. salt
¾ c. red wine vinegar
¼ c. onion, grated
2 c. canola oil
5 Tbs. poppy seeds
½ tsp. coriander, ground

Ingredients for salad:

1 lemon, juiced
1 c. water
2 bananas, peeled, sliced
1 red apple, cored, sliced
2 pears, peeled, sliced
1 c. seedless green grapes
1 c. seedless purple grapes
8 plums, pitted, quartered
1 pt. fresh strawberries, stems removed
1 melon, peeled, cut into med. chunks
2 peaches, peeled, pitted, sliced

Directions for poppy seed dressing:

1. In large bowl, place honey, dry mustard, salt, vinegar, and onion; stir together.
2. With electric mixer, on medium speed, slowly add all the oil; beat well.
3. When all combined and nicely thickened, add coriander and poppy seeds; beat 3 minutes longer.
4. Pour into lidded containers and refrigerate.

5. Stir again before using.

Directions for salad:

1. Use the freshest fruit possible.
2. In large bowl, combine lemon juice and water.
3. Soak bananas, apples, and pears in this liquid to prevent discoloring.
4. Remove fruit from solution; combine all fruit in a large mixing bowl; fold gently to mix.
5. Spoon fruit mixture into a bowl or onto individual plates lined with curly lettuce leaves.
6. When ready to serve, pour dressing over the top.

Tomato and Avocado Salad

This is a tasty, colorful, and easy-to-make salad that everyone will enjoy.

Ingredients:

2 tomatoes, cored
1 avocado, peeled, pitted, diced
2 Tbs. lemon juice
1 red onion, sliced
    salt and pepper, to taste

Directions:

1. Slice tomato in half and squeeze seeds into a bowl; discard.
2. Dice tomato; transfer to medium bowl.
3. Add avocado and onion; mix well.
4. Add lemon juice; season with salt and pepper; mix gently.
5. Chill until ready to serve.
6. May be served on lettuce leaves if desired.

Yields: 2 servings.

Beef and Broccoli Salad

This is a delicious salad. Serve with bread and dessert to make a wonderful light meal.

Ingredients for salad:

8	slices beef tenderloin steak (1-inch pieces)
1	head broccoli, florets, cut stems into chunks
1	pkg. mixed baby greens (8 oz.)
1½	red bell pepper, seeded, thinly sliced
4	scallions, sliced diagonally into 1-inch pieces
1	c. pea pods, sliced diagonally
1	c. carrots, shredded
12	hot cherry peppers or pepperoncini, chopped
2	Tbs. cilantro leaves, chopped
	salt and pepper, to taste
	olive oil

Ingredients for dressing:

¼	prepared sweet and sour sauce
1	pc. gingerroot, finely chopped (1-inch)
1	lime, juiced
2	Tbs. rice wine vinegar or white vinegar
1	tsp. crushed red pepper flakes, to taste
¼	c. olive oil

Directions:

1. Preheat grill pan over high heat.
2. Season steak with salt and pepper.
3. Sprinkle grill pan with olive oil.
4. Grill meat 3 to 5 minutes per side for medium rare to medium-well doneness.
5. Remove meat; let stand for 10 minutes.
6. In medium saucepan, bring 1 inch of water to boil; add pinch of salt and broccoli stem pieces.

7. Steam 2 minutes; add broccoli florets and steam 3 minutes longer, just until cooked to firm stage.
8. Drain broccoli in colander; run cold water over it to cool.
9. When ready to serve, arrange greens as desired.
10. Arrange broccoli and other vegetables on top of greens; sprinkle cilantro over top.
11. In small bowl, combine sweet and sour sauce, ginger, lime juice, vinegar, and crushed red pepper flakes; whisk in olive oil.
12. Slice steaks in thin strips and arrange over top of salad.
13. Drizzle each salad with dressing and season with salt and pepper to taste.

Fresh Peach and Kiwi Salad

This is a tasty salad in which to enjoy the great pure taste of the combined fruits.

Ingredients:

    6 peaches, peeled, thickly sliced
    5 kiwi fruit, peeled, sliced
    3 oranges, juiced
    1 lemon, juiced
       sugar, to taste
       mint leaves, for garnish

Directions:

1. Place peach and kiwi slices in a medium bowl.
2. Add citrus juices and sugar to taste.
3. Fold very gently to blend.
4. Place in refrigerator and chill several hours.
5. When ready to serve, spoon into serving dishes and top with mint leaves.

Fruit Salad

This is a unique fresh fruit salad. The combination of fresh apricots, strawberries, and kiwis is unusual and very refreshing with the bits of fresh mint to top it off.

Ingredients:

    2   c. fresh apricots, pitted, sliced
    1¾ c. fresh strawberries, hulled, halved
    1¾ c. kiwi fruit, pared, sliced
    ¼   c. apricot nectar
    ⅓   c. coconut flakes, lightly toasted
    1   Tbs. fresh mint, finely chopped

Directions:

1. In large bowl, combine fruits and nectar, mixing lightly.
2. Gently add coconut flakes by tossing lightly.
3. Cover and place in refrigerator to chill.
4. When ready to serve, gently scoop fruit mixture into small fruit bowls and garnish with bits of fresh mint.

Confetti Chopped Salad

This colorful and healthy salad is a perfect accompaniment for grilled beef.

Ingredients:

    1 red bell pepper, seeded, diced
    1 yellow bell pepper, seeded, diced
    1 green bell pepper, seeded, diced
    2 Roma tomatoes, diced
    1 sm. zucchini, diced
    ½ cucumber, seedless, unpeeled, diced
    2 Tbs. fresh parsley, chopped
    2 scallions, leave 3 inches green, thin diagonal slices
    4 Tbs. olive oil
    3 Tbs. red wine vinegar

½ tsp. sugar
1 ripe avocado, peeled, pitted, diced
2 Tbs. fresh lemon juice
   salt and freshly ground black pepper, to taste

Directions:

1. In large bowl, combine peppers, tomato, zucchini, cucumber, parsley, and scallions.
2. In small bowl, whisk together olive oil, vinegar, sugar; and salt and pepper to taste.
3. Pour over salad and toss well.
4. In small bowl, toss avocado with lemon juice.
5. When ready to serve, sprinkle salad with avocado mixture.

Waldorf Salad

This is a refreshing crunchy salad that my mother used to make for a change of pace in our Sunday meal.

Ingredients:

2 c. red apples, cored, diced
¼ c. lemon juice
1 c. celery, chopped
1 c. nuts, coarsely chopped
¾ c. raisins
1 c. mayonnaise

Directions:

1. In small bowl, combine apples with lemon juice; set aside.
2. In medium bowl, add celery, apples, and raisins; mix well.
3. Add nuts and mayonnaise; mix well.
4. Chill in refrigerator.
5. Line individual plates with lettuce leaves.
6. Spoon chilled mixture on top of lettuce.
7. Sprinkle with additional nuts if desired.

Two Blue Cheese Salad

This is a great combination of fresh blueberries, blue cheese, and raspberries. The pecans add even more flavor as well as texture.

Ingredients for salad:

> 1 head lettuce, butter or Boston bib
> ¾ c. blue cheese, crumbled
> ¾ c. pecan halves
> 1 Tbs. olive oil
> ¾ c. blueberries

Ingredients for dressing:

> ¾ c. raspberries, whole, fresh or frozen
> ½ c. raspberry vinegar
> ½ c. honey
> 1 c. olive oil

Directions for salad:

1. Wash, drain, and break apart lettuce, including tiny leaves in the middle.
2. Place on serving dishes.
3. Pour olive oil in skillet; lightly brown pecan halves; set aside to cool.
4. Place blue cheese, pecan halves, and blueberries on top of lettuce and drizzle dressing over all.

Directions for dressing:

1. In blender or food processor, combine raspberries, vinegar, and honey.
2. Turn on blender; slowly add oil. The dressing will be slightly thick.
3. Serve as directed above.

Greek Salad

My daughter, Mikayla, loves to make this salad, and the entire family enjoys eating it. Be sure to use the best Greek olives for better flavor.

Ingredients for salad:

- 5 c. spinach, torn into bite-size pieces
- 4 c. Boston lettuce, torn into bite-size pieces
- ¼ c. green onions, sliced
- 3 med. tomatoes, cut into wedges
- 1 med. cucumber, sliced
- 24 Greek olives, pitted
- ½ c. feta cheese, crumbled

Ingredients for lemon dressing:

- ¼ c. olive oil
- 3 Tbs. lemon juice
- 1½ tsp. Dijon mustard
- ⅛ tsp. pepper
  - salt, to taste

Directions:

1. In large salad bowl, combine and toss together spinach leaves, lettuce, and green onions.
2. Mix in tomatoes, cucumber, and olives.
3. Sprinkle in the cheese.
4. Place olive oil and lemon juice into a tightly covered container; shake well to break up oil.
5. Add mustard, pepper, and salt to taste.
6. Shake until well blended.
7. When ready to serve, pour the dressing over the salad ingredients and toss together.
8. Serve with your favorite bread or meal.

Onion Potato Salad

Red potatoes have great flavor and so do Walla Walla sweet onions. Add dill pickles, green olives, and Dijon mustard, and you have a fantastic potato salad.

Ingredients:

    3   lb. red potatoes, peeled, cooked
    1   lg. Walla Walla onion, peeled
    1   c. celery, sliced
    ⅓   c. pickle relish
    20 lg. pimento stuffed olives, sliced
    1½ c. mayonnaise
    2   tsp. Dijon mustard
    2   Tbs. white wine vinegar
        salt and pepper, to taste

Directions:

    1. Cube potatoes; slice onions into thin slices.
    2. In large bowl, combine potatoes, onions, celery, olives, and pickle relish.
    3. In small bowl, blend mayonnaise, vinegar, and mustard well.
    4. Pour over potatoes and lightly combine so as not to break up potatoes.
    5. Season with salt and pepper to taste.
    6. Cover; refrigerate several hours or overnight to blend flavors before serving.

Tomato and Onion Salad

Fresh tomatoes and sweet onion slices make a great salad by themselves, or you can add them to greens.

Ingredients:

    1 firm tomato
    1 med. Walla Walla sweet onion
        dressing of your choice

Directions:

1. Cut tomatoes into ¼-inch slices.
2. Thinly slice onion and place alternately in salad bowl with tomatoes.
3. Pour dressing over top.
4. Cover and refrigerate to let tomatoes and onions marinate.
5. Serve as they are, or add to select salad greens with halved boiled eggs on the side.

Layered Salad

This is a very easy-to-make recipe, and it is nice to have a salad that can be made ahead of your guest's arrival.

Ingredients:

3 c. iceberg lettuce, torn
1 can kidney beans, drained, rinsed (15 oz.)
2 c. broccoli florets, cut apart if large
2 c. carrots, sliced
2 c. red pepper chunks, cut into 1-inch pieces
1 c. mayonnaise
1 Tbs. plus 2 tsp. buttermilk
  salad dressing mix
  green onions, sliced, for garnish
  cherry tomatoes, halved, for garnish
  parsley sprigs, for garnish

Directions:

1. In large salad bowl, layer half the lettuce, beans, broccoli, carrots, and red peppers; repeat with other half of vegetables.
2. In small bowl, combine mayonnaise, buttermilk, and salad dressing mix; spoon over top of salad.
3. Garnish with green onions, cherry tomato halves, and parsley sprigs.

Asparagus Salad

Nothing is better than fresh asparagus! This salad is a nice addition to a holiday or special meal. Enjoy!

Ingredients:

¼ c. white wine vinegar
1 Tbs. shallots, minced
2 tsp. Dijon mustard
¾ tsp. salt
½ tsp. freshly ground pepper
½ c. canola oil
¼ c. walnut oil
2 lb. asparagus, trimmed, steamed until just tender
⅓ c. walnuts, toasted, chopped
1 Tbs. fresh parsley leaves, chopped
   salt and freshly ground black pepper

Directions:

1. In large bowl, whisk together vinegar, shallots, mustard, salt, and pepper.
2. While continuing to whisk, add oil in a very thin stream, whisking constantly.
3. Whisk in walnut oil.
4. Place asparagus on platter; pour dressing over top.
5. Garnish with walnuts and parsley.
6. Taste; adjust seasonings if necessary.
7. Serve immediately.

German Potato Salad

We have always found this German-style salad excellent for any occasion. It is such a change of pace, as it is served warm and needs no refrigeration.

Ingredients:

6 lg. potatoes, unpeeled, boiled, chopped
1 Vidalia sweet onion, peeled, chopped
3 eggs, hard-boiled, chopped

¾ lb. bacon, fried crisp, crumbled, reserve drippings
½ tsp. celery salt
⅓ c. sugar
    salt and pepper, to taste
    tarragon vinegar, equal to the amount of bacon
    drippings

Directions:

1. In medium bowl, combine potatoes, onions, and eggs.
2. Sprinkle with salt, pepper, and celery salt; set aside.
3. In small pan, measure bacon drippings; bring to boil.
4. Add equal amount of tarragon vinegar, and sugar.
5. Boil for 1 minute; pour over potato mix.
6. Taste and adjust seasonings if necessary.
7. Crumble bacon and add to mixture.
8. Toss lightly; serve warm or at room temperature.

Chickpea and Red Onion Salad

This simple salad is both easy to make and delicious. It is a quick and elegant salad for company.

Ingredients:

2 c. canned chickpeas
3 Tbs. ready-made pesto sauce
1 Tbs. olive oil
1 Tbs. lemon juice
¾ c. red onions, chopped

Directions:

1. Drain and rinse chickpeas.
2. In medium bowl, whisk pesto, oil, and lemon juice together.
3. Add chickpeas and red onions; toss lightly.
4. Note: This salad is best served at room temperature.

Coconut Mango Rice Salad

Cilantro and mint add a nice touch to this coconut-flavored rice salad.

Ingredients:

5   green onions, sliced
3   garlic cloves, minced
½   c. cilantro leaves, loosely packed
½   c. mint leaves, loosely packed
½   c. fresh parsley leaves, loosely packed
1   can coconut milk (14 oz.)
1½ c. long-grain white rice
1½ tsp. sea salt
1   Tbs. olive oil
1   med. mango, peeled, pitted, chopped
¼   c. red onions, chopped
1   garlic clove, minced
1   Tbs. sugar
¼   c. red wine vinegar
1   c. olive oil
¼   tsp. sea salt
¼   tsp. fresh ground pepper
2   med. ripe peaches, chopped
1   med. red pepper, chopped
1½ c. English cucumber, chopped

Directions:

1. In food processor, combine ¼ of sliced green onions, garlic, cilantro, mint, and parsley.
2. Pulse to finely chop; scrape into glass bowl.
3. Add coconut milk, mixing well.
4. Measure and add enough water to make 4 cups.
5. Whisk well and set aside.
6. In large pot, over medium-high heat, add rice, salt, and oil; stir to coat.

7. Add milk mixture; bring to a boil.
8. Reduce heat to medium-low and cover; cook 18 minutes.
9. Remove from heat; let stand covered 5 minutes.
10. Turn rice into large bowl; toss well to cool and separate.
11. Place in refrigerator, stirring often to help cool.
12. Note: If serving right away, toss with dressing to coat. If serving later, cover rice mixture and dressing separately.
13. Add desired amount of dressing right before serving.

Directions for dressing:

1. In food processor, combine mango, onion, garlic, sugar, and red wine vinegar; purée until smooth.
2. While machine is running slowly, add oil in a very thin stream.
3. Add salt and pepper; pulse to combine.
4. To the rice, add peaches, red pepper, and cucumber.

One-Cup Coconut Salad

This is an easy and delicious salad.

Ingredients:

1 c. mandarin oranges, drained
1 c. coconut
1 c. pineapple tidbits, drained
1 c. mini marshmallows
1 c. sour cream

Directions:

1. In large bowl, combine all ingredients.
2. Prepare several hours before serving and chill.

Cucumber Salad

My mom made this the best salad ever by using sour cream and yogurt mixed together and combining with sliced cucumbers.

Ingredients:

- 3 med. cucumbers, peeled, halved lengthwise, sliced
- 2 Tbs. kosher salt
- ¼ c. sour cream
- ¼ c. plain yogurt
- 3 Tbs. fresh dill, chopped
- 1 Tbs. white distilled vinegar
  freshly ground black pepper

Directions:

1. Place cucumbers in a large bowl and salt; set aside at room temperature for 30 minutes.
2. Transfer cucumbers to a colander, drain and rinse thoroughly under cold running water; make sure all salt is rinsed off.
3. Set aside to drain for 10 minutes.
4. Place on paper towels and press down on the cucumbers to extract as much liquid as possible.
5. In small bowl, combine sour cream, yogurt, dill, vinegar, and season with pepper, to taste.
6. Transfer cucumbers to a large bowl and mix with the dressing to serve.

Did You Know? . . . .

Did you know that Chinese family names often begin with a sign that means "mother"? It is a nice way of honoring their mom's long past.

Mother's Day Delights Cookbook
A Collection of Mother's Day Recipes
Cookbook Delights Holiday Series-Book 5

Side Dishes

Table of Contents

Page

Hush Puppies

Hush puppies are often served with fish, and are always best served hot. Legend has it that campfire cooks threw them to hungry dogs, as they were told, "Hush, puppies!"

Ingredients:

¼ c. flour
2 tsp. baking soda
½ tsp. salt
¾ c. cornmeal
1 egg
½ c. milk
1 green onion, finely minced
1 pimento, finely minced
3 Tbs. parsley, finely minced
½ tsp. garlic powder
   cayenne pepper
   canola oil, for frying

Directions:

1. In large bowl, combine flour, baking soda, salt, and cornmeal.
2. Add egg, milk, and seasonings; stir just until moistened.
3. In large skillet, preheat oil.
4. Drop batter from a spoon into hot oil; cook until light brown.
5. Remove from oil and drain on paper towels.
6. Serve while warm.
7. Note: These may also be squeezed from a pastry bag, fitted with a star tip, directly into the hot oil, forming pretzel shapes, which are light and crisp. The flavor is improved if the oil has previously had shrimp or fish fried in it.

Lentil Vegetable Rice

This is a very nutritional dish that can be served for everyone, including the vegetarians. Serve with your favorite meat, poultry, or fish.

Ingredients:

1½ c. brown lentils, washed, picked over
1   qt. water
1   bay leaf
3   stalks celery, sliced
2   med. carrots, sliced
1   bunch scallions, sliced
2½ c. tomatoes, diced
½   lb. zucchini, diced
1   tsp. ground coriander
½   tsp. cumin
¼   tsp. cayenne pepper
½   tsp. black pepper
½   tsp. salt
4   lg. garlic cloves, minced
¼   c. fresh cilantro, chopped
1   lemon, juiced
2   c. brown rice, cooked

Directions:

1. In large saucepan, cook lentils with water and bay leaf for 20 minutes, until just tender; remove bay leaf.
2. Add celery, carrots, scallions, tomatoes, zucchini, spices, salt and peppers; mix well.
3. Cook 15 minutes, or until vegetables are crisp-tender.
4. Stir in garlic, cilantro, and lemon juice.
5. Serve over hot cooked rice.

Pasta with Roasted Vegetables

Roasted vegetables are so nutritious and these add a wonderful flavor to the dish.

Ingredients:

    3 med. zucchini, cut in half lengthwise, sliced
    1 med. red onion, sliced into crescents
    1 leek (white part only), thinly sliced, rings separated
    1 med. red bell pepper, cut into 1 inch pieces
    1 med. yellow bell pepper, cut into 1 inch pieces
    1 sm. eggplant, cut in half lengthwise, sliced
    3 Tbs. balsamic vinegar, divided
    1 Tbs. olive oil
    5 med. garlic cloves, finely chopped
    1 tsp. salt
    1 tsp. pepper
    2 c. penne pasta, cooked
    ½ lb. boneless, skinless chicken, cooked, cubed
    ½ c. chicken broth
    1 Tbs. fresh basil leaves, chopped
    1 lg. ripe avocados, seeded, peeled, cut into 8 slices
       fresh basil leaves, for garnish

Directions:

1. Preheat oven to 375 degrees F.
2. In large roasting pan sprayed with nonstick cooking spray, combine all vegetables.
3. In small bowl, blend 2 tablespoons balsamic vinegar, oil, garlic, salt, and pepper.
4. Pour over vegetables and toss to coat; spread evenly in pan.
5. Bake 30 to 35 minutes, stirring twice.
6. Add remaining balsamic vinegar.
7. In large bowl, toss cooked pasta, roasted vegetables, chicken, chicken broth, and basil.
8. When ready to serve, place a slice of avocado and a fresh basil leaf on top of each bowl of pasta.

Creamed Mushrooms

These creamed mushrooms make an excellent side dish for any of your meals.

Ingredients:

1½ lb. fresh white mushrooms
1   lb. fresh exotic mushrooms, such as porcini, chanterelles, or portobello
½   lb. shallots, chopped
⅜   c. butter, unsalted
2   Tbs. cognac
⅔   c. chicken broth
⅔   c. heavy cream
1   Tbs. paprika, preferably mild Hungarian
½   c. packed fresh flat leafed parsley, minced
⅔   c. sour cream

Directions:

1. Cut white mushrooms lengthwise into ½-inch wedges; chop exotic mushrooms.
2. In a deep, heavy 12-inch skillet, cook shallots in butter over low heat, stirring until softened.
3. Stir in cognac; increase heat to medium.
4. Cook, while stirring for 1 minute.
5. Add mushrooms; while stirring, cook 2 more minutes.
6. Add broth, heavy cream, paprika, and salt and pepper, to taste; simmer, stirring occasionally, until liquid is reduced to 1½ cups.
7. Remove skillet from heat.
8. Stir in parsley and sour cream.
9. Note: This may be made 1 day ahead. Cool completely before covering and refrigerate.
10. Reheat mushrooms; stir in parsley and sour cream.

Potato Wedges with Aioli

This is a delicious potato dish to serve with any main dish and will be appreciated by all.

Ingredients for potatoes:

    6 lg. white potatoes, washed, leave whole
    1 tsp. salt
    4 Tbs. flour
    1 tsp. paprika
    ½ tsp. cayenne pepper
    2 Tbs. olive oil or melted butter
       salt, to taste
       freshly ground black pepper, to serve

Ingredients for aioli:

    2 garlic cloves, crushed
    ¾ c. whole egg mayonnaise
       pinch of salt
       lemon juice, to taste

Directions for potatoes:

1. Lightly grease a shallow baking dish.
2. In large saucepan, place potatoes in boiling, salted water.
3. Cook 15 to 20 minutes, until just tender but not too soft.
4. Drain, peel, and slice each potato into quarters lengthwise to form wedges; pat dry with paper towel.
5. Preheat oven to 400 degrees F.
6. In large bowl, combine salt, flour, paprika, and cayenne pepper.
7. Toss wedges first in oil or butter to coat, then in flour mixture.

8. Bake 20 minutes, turning after 10 minutes, until crispy and golden brown.
9. Serve sprinkled with salt and pepper or topped with a little salsa, accompanied by aioli.

Directions for aioli:

1. In small bowl, whip crushed garlic into mayonnaise.
2. Add a pinch of salt and a generous squeeze of lemon juice to taste.
3. Try adding sweet chili sauce or zest of lime for something different.
4. Serve at room temperature.

Stewed Cabbage

This is a delicious way to serve cabbage at your meals.

Ingredients:

¼ c. butter
2 onions, chopped
1 stalk celery, chopped
2 cloves garlic, chopped
1 med. head cabbage, cut into squares
1 can tomatoes, stewed, with liquid (14 oz.)
salt and pepper, to taste

Directions:

1. In large saucepan, over medium heat, melt butter.
2. Add onion, celery, and garlic; sauté 3 to 5 minutes, or until translucent.
3. Stir in cabbage, reduce heat to low; simmer 15 minutes.
4. Pour in tomatoes; season with salt and pepper to taste; mix well.
5. Cover; increase heat to medium; cook 30 to 40 minutes or until cabbage is tender.

Onion Bread Pudding

This is a tasty side dish that can be served at any meal in place of the traditional dressing.

Ingredients:

- 1   Tbs. butter
- 1   Tbs. canola oil
- 1½ c. sweet onion, finely chopped
- 4   slices stale bread
- 1   c. milk
- ¼   c. cream
- 2   eggs
- 1   tsp. hot sauce
- 2   Tbs. fresh parsley, chopped
- 1   tsp. sesame seeds, toasted
        salt and pepper, to taste

Directions:

1. Preheat oven to 325 degrees F.
2. In small skillet, over low heat, melt butter with oil.
3. Cook onion, 30 minutes, until tender and golden; do not brown.
4. Butter each bread slice lightly on both sides.
5. Cut into cubes and spread half of them over the bottom of a large, buttered casserole dish.
6. Sprinkle cooked onions over the bread.
7. Top with remaining bread cubes.
8. In small bowl, whisk together milk, cream, eggs, hot sauce, parsley, and salt and pepper, to taste.
9. Pour over bread mixture.
10. Sprinkle with sesame seeds.
11. Bake 25 to 30 minutes, or until knife inserted in middle comes out clean.
12. Serve hot.

Potatoes Au Gratin

Potatoes au gratin is a version of scalloped potatoes with Cheddar cheese melted in. Most of our family prefers au gratin potatoes, so we rotate them in frequently.

Ingredients:

2 lb. potatoes, peeled
2 Tbs. butter
¼ c. flour
2 c. milk, heated
⅓ tsp. salt
¼ tsp. pepper
½ lb. Cheddar cheese, shredded
¾ c. dry bread crumbs
2 Tbs. butter, melted

Directions:

1. Preheat oven to 375 degrees F.
2. Lightly spray with cooking oil, a 9 x 1-inch casserole dish.
3. In large saucepan, cook potatoes in boiling salted water until tender; drain. Cool slightly and dice.
4. In medium saucepan, melt butter; stir in flour.
5. Add milk; cook and stir 20 minutes, until smooth and thick.
6. Add seasonings, stir in cheese; blend.
7. Pour sauce over potatoes; stir to blend.
8. Spoon mixture into prepared casserole dish.
9. In small bowl, combine crumbs and butter, stir until blended.
10. Sprinkle over potatoes.
11. Bake 25 minutes, or until bubbly hot.
12. Remove from oven.
13. Serve with your favorite meat, poultry, or fish.

Zucchini Side Dish

A rich blend of onions, zucchini, and bacon in a cheese sauce makes this side dish a welcome addition to your meal.

Ingredients:

>3 med. zucchini, sliced
>1 med. onion, diced
>5 slices bacon, diced
>½ c. cream
>2 Tbs. Parmesan cheese, freshly grated
>1½ Tbs. dried basil

Directions:

1. In large skillet, over medium heat, add bacon and onion; sauté 5 minutes.
2. Arrange zucchini on top of onion and bacon; cook, covered, for another 5 minutes.
3. In small bowl, combine cream, Parmesan cheese, and basil.
4. Pour over zucchini mixture.
5. Cover; cook 2 additional minutes.

Squash Bake

Baked squash is always a delight for a meal, but this one is even more delicious with the cherries and nuts added.

Ingredients:

>2 acorn squash
>¼ c. butter, melted
>½ c. dried tart cherries
>¼ c. pecans, chopped
>3 Tbs. light brown sugar, firmly packed
>½ tsp. cinnamon

Directions:

1. Preheat oven to 350 degrees F.
2. Cut each squash in half; remove seeds and fiber.
3. Place cut side down in baking pan with small amount of water in bottom.
4. Bake 35 to 40 minutes, or until squash is tender and can be pierced with a fork.
5. In small saucepan, combine butter, cherries, pecans, brown sugar, and cinnamon.
6. Heat over low heat until butter melts.
7. Remove squash from oven; fill center of each piece of squash with cherry mixture.

Lentil Basil Couscous

This is a delicious side dish that will complement any of your main dishes with its nutritional value.

Ingredients:

2   Tbs. butter
1   med. onion, chopped
1½ c .water
1   c. vegetable broth
1   c. brown lentils, rinsed, drained
1   bay leaf
1   c. whole wheat couscous
1   med. tomato, coarsely chopped
½   c. fresh basil, chopped

Directions:

1. In large saucepan, over medium heat, melt butter; sauté onions 2 to 3 minutes, or until tender.
2. Stir in water, broth, lentils, and bay leaf; bring to boil; stir in couscous and tomato.
3. Reduce heat to low; cover and simmer 30 to 45 minutes, or until lentils are soft but not mushy.
4. Ladle into a serving dish; sprinkle with basil.

Baked Potatoes with Stuffing

We have two vegetarians in the family, and tofu adds protein to baked potatoes. Add your favorite seasoning to taste.

Ingredients:

- 4 potatoes, baked
- 12 oz. tofu, pressed
- 1 c. cheese, grated or diced
- ½ tsp. salt
- 1½ Tbs. butter
- 1 onion, minced
- 1 Tbs. oil
  - minced chives, to taste
  - pepper, to taste

Directions:

1. Preheat oven to 350 degrees F.
2. Lightly grease baking sheet.
3. Cut potatoes lengthwise and scoop out shells.
4. Spoon 1 cup of potato into a bowl; reserve remainder.
5. Mash tofu and cheese with potato in a bowl.
6. Season with salt and pepper.
7. In small skillet, melt butter; sauté onion until light brown.
8. Stir into potato tofu mixture; divide mixture among potato shells.
9. Bake 30 minutes or until nicely browned.
10. Top with butter, sour cream, and minced chives.
11. Serve with your favorite main dish along with a salad and fresh bread.

Yields: 6 to 8 servings.

Boston Baked Beans

If you have only had baked beans from a can, you don't know what you are missing. This recipe is great. They do take a long time, but they are easy and inexpensive.

Ingredients:

    2 c. dried beans
    ½ lb. salt pork
    4 Tbs. thick black molasses
    1 tsp. mustard
       salt to taste

Directions:

1. In medium bowl, soak beans overnight in enough cold water to cover.
2. In the morning, drain beans; add a quart of fresh water.
3. Pour beans into a large saucepan; over low heat, simmer 45 minutes, or until beans begin to soften; drain.
4. Preheat oven to 300 degrees F.
5. Score salt pork rind and put half of the pork in the bottom of a bean pot.
6. Pour in beans.
7. In small bowl, combine molasses, mustard, and salt with a little hot water; pour over beans.
8. Add enough hot water to cover.
9. Place remaining salt pork on top; cover.
10. Bake 6 or 7 hours.
11. Add a little hot water from time to time as the beans absorb water.
12. Keep lid on bean pot until last hour of cooking; uncover and allow beans and pork on the top to brown.
13. Serve hot or cold if desired.

Wild Rice with Mushrooms

Wild rice is always delicious and makes an excellent versatile side dish.

Ingredients:

    1 c. wild rice
    2 Tbs. butter or oil
    1 Tbs. onion, grated
    1 Tbs. parsley, finely chopped
    1 Tbs. chives, finely chopped
    ¾ lb. fresh mushrooms, thinly sliced
    1 pinch of nutmeg
       salt and pepper, to taste

Directions:

1. In small saucepan, cook wild rice; drain.
2. In medium saucepan over medium heat, melt butter; stir in onion, parsley, and chives; sauté for 3 minutes; reduce heat to low.
3. Add mushrooms; cook 5 minutes, stirring constantly; season to taste with salt, pepper, and nutmeg.
4. Stir into rice and serve.

Sweet Potato Cakes

These sweet potato cakes are delicious as a side dish for your main meal. Serve with a dollop of sour cream if desired.

Ingredients:

    1 lg. sweet potato, grated
    ¼ c. sweet onion, grated
    2 Tbs. green onion, chopped
    1 egg
    1 Tbs. flour
    1 tsp. Chinese parsley, chopped
    ½ tsp. lemon juice

¾ tsp. salt
1 dash white pepper
1 c. macadamia nut oil or canola oil

Directions:

1. In large bowl, combine potato, onions, egg, and flour.
2. Add parsley, lemon juice, salt and pepper, to taste; mix well until ingredients adhere together; form into 3-inch patties.
3. In large skillet, over medium heat, heat oil; fry until light brown and cooked through.

Veggies and Rice

This is a flavorful rice dish that is easy to put together and delicious enough for company or family to enjoy.

Ingredients:

1 c. baby corn
1 celery stalk, chopped
1 carrot, chopped
1 c. green peas
½ onion, cubed
½ c. mushrooms, sliced
2 green onions, chopped, reserve some for garnish
2 garlic cloves, chopped
1 sm. piece fresh ginger, chopped
4 c. brown rice, cooked
   soy sauce and olive oil, to taste

Directions:

1. In lightly greased large skillet, over medium heat, add corn, celery, carrots, and peas; sauté until crisp.
2. Add onion, mushrooms, green onion, garlic, and ginger along with soy sauce; continue to sauté.
3. Add rice; sauté with additional oil and soy sauce until done.
4. Place in serving dish; top with green onions.

Potatoes with Onion Bits

These mashed, red potatoes are cooked with the skins on for the added flavor, texture, and vitamins. Adding the onion gives them an "out of the ordinary" taste.

Ingredients:

> 1   sm. onion, peeled, diced
> 1   Tbs. olive oil
> 12 med. red potatoes, washed, leave skins on
> ⅔ c. milk
> ½ c. butter, softened
> 1   tsp. salt
> ½ tsp. pepper
>   paprika, for garnish

Directions:

1. In small saucepan, place onion and oil.
2. Sauté onion just until soft but not browned.
3. Place potatoes in 6-quart or larger kettle.
4. Add enough water to cover potatoes.
5. Heat to boiling; reduce heat.
6. Cover and simmer 20 to 30 minutes, or until potatoes are tender; drain.
7. Shake pan with potatoes over low heat to dry. This will make the mashed potatoes fluffier.
8. Add butter, salt, pepper, and milk.
9. Mash vigorously until potatoes are light and fluffy.
10. Sprinkle onions over mashed potatoes.
11. Stir just enough to incorporate them.
12. Place in serving bowl.
13. Top with dots of butter and a shake or two of paprika for garnish.

Yields: 8 to 10 servings.

Mother's Day Delights Cookbook
A Collection of Mother's Day Recipes
Cookbook Delights Holiday Series-Book 5

Soups

Table of Contents

Page

Cream of Mushroom Soup

This rich and heavy soup can be a meal in itself. When possible, I try to use a variety of mushrooms for a varied, interesting flavor.

Ingredients:

3	lb. mushrooms, any or combined variety
1½	c. butter
3	tsp. fresh lemon juice
3	sm. onions, diced
1	c. flour
10½	c. vegetable broth
3	tsp. salt
¾	tsp. pepper
3	c. heavy cream
	chives or chopped green onions, for garnish

Directions:

1. Remove stem end of mushrooms; set aside.
2. Slice mushroom caps thinly.
3. In Dutch oven, or soup pot, melt butter over medium-high heat.
4. Add mushroom caps and lemon juice.
5. Sauté until mushrooms are tender.
6. Reduce heat to low.
7. With a slotted spoon transfer mushrooms to a small plate.
8. Add onion and mushroom stems to Dutch oven.
9. Cook until onions are tender.
10. Stir in flour until blended; cook 1 minute, stirring constantly.
11. Gradually stir in broth, stirring constantly until thickened; cool to lukewarm.
12. In food processor or blender, process until is puréed. This may have to be done in batches.

13. Return to Dutch oven.
14. Add salt, pepper, cream, and sautéed mushrooms.
15. Reheat until warm.
16. Serve garnished with chives or green onions.

Clam Corn Chowder

This is delicious chowder that the whole family enjoys. Serve it with some fresh crusty bread or crackers.

Ingredients:

1 med. onion, chopped
4 Tbs. flour, divided
¼ c. butter
6 slices crisp bacon, crumbled
3 cans clams, chopped with juice (8 oz. ea.)
1 c. fresh corn, shaved from cob
2 c. potatoes, diced
½ tsp. salt
¼ tsp. fresh pepper
2 c. heavy cream

Directions:

1. In large pot, sauté onion in butter; sprinkle 2 tablespoons flour over mixture and stir.
2. Add bacon, clams, corn, and potatoes.
3. Season to taste with salt and pepper.
4. In measuring cup mix remaining flour with a little warm water to dissolve it.
5. Add mixture to pot and bring just to boiling.
6. Reduce heat and cover; simmer 30 minutes. If you want a thicker base, add a bit more flour mixed with warm water.
7. Remove from heat, ladle into serving bowls.
8. Serve with oyster crackers, fresh bread, and a salad.

Ham and Bean Soup

This is a flavorful ham soup that the whole family will enjoy sharing together. For a quick, light meal, serve it with some fresh crusty bread.

Ingredients:

   1 lb. dried navy beans, sorted
   1 ham bone, with ample meat attached
   2 onions, chopped
   1 Tbs. fresh garlic, minced
   2 green onions, chopped
   2 carrots, chopped
   1 lg. potato
   2 celery spears, chopped
   ½ tsp. coarsely ground black pepper
   ½ tsp. garlic powder
      salt, to taste

Directions:

   1. In large pot, soak beans overnight in warm water.
   2. Parboil by bringing water covering beans to a boil for 5 minutes; drain and cover again with fresh water. This process helps to remove gaseous action of beans.
   3. Bring beans to boil with enough water so that there is 3 inches above the beans.
   4. Add potato and ham bone; cover and cook 1 hour. Add more water during cooking if necessary.
   5. In small skillet sauté onions, garlic, and green onions; add to beans.
   6. Remove 1 cup of beans and the potato from pot.
   7. Mash beans with boiled potato; return to pot.
   8. Add spices to taste; cook another 15 minutes.
   9. Remove ham bone, slice meat off the bone; add back to soup.

10. Simmer 30 to 45 minutes more, or until beans are very tender.
11. Remove from heat.
12. Ladle into serving bowls.
13. Serve with some warm crusty bread if desired.

Avgolemono Soup

This is one of my very favorite Greek soups. I love the combination of chicken broth and lemon. It is also great without the lemon. Even the children enjoy its refreshing taste!

Ingredients:

12 c. homemade or canned chicken broth
1⅛ c. long-grain white rice
24 egg yolks
1   c. fresh lemon juice
     kosher salt
     black pepper, freshly ground

Directions:

1. In medium saucepan, bring stock to boil.
2. Stir in rice; cook 15 to 20 minutes, or until tender.
3. In large bowl, beat egg yolks and lemon juice together.
4. Slowly ladle half of the hot broth into the yolks to temper them, whisking constantly.
5. Whisk egg yolk mixture into the broth and place over low heat.
6. Cook, stirring constantly, until thickened. Do not boil.
7. Season with salt and pepper, to taste.
8. Ladle into individual serving bowls.

African Peanut Soup

This is a thick, hearty soup that is delicious. Serve it topped with plenty of chopped scallions and chopped peanuts.

Ingredients:

    2 c. onion, chopped
    1 Tbs. canola oil
    ½ tsp. cayenne pepper
    1 tsp. fresh ginger, peeled, grated
    1 c. carrots, chopped
    2 c. sweet potatoes, chopped
    4 c. vegetable stock or water
    2 c. tomato juice
    1 c. peanut butter, smooth
    1 Tbs. sugar
    ¼ c. scallions, chopped
    ½ c. peanuts, roasted

Directions:

1. In large Dutch oven, sauté onion in oil until translucent.
2. Stir in cayenne and ginger.
3. Add carrots; sauté a couple minutes more.
4. Mix in sweet potatoes and stock, bring to boil; simmer 15 minutes, until vegetables are tender.
5. In blender or food processor, purée vegetables with tomato juice and some cooking liquid if necessary. Return purée to the pot.
6. Stir in peanut butter until smooth. Taste for sweetness; add sugar if necessary.
7. Reheat gently.
8. Add more water, stock, or tomato juice to make a thinner soup if desired.

Minestrone Soup

This is one of those hearty, delicious soups that can be made with or without the meat so it will serve vegetarians also.

Ingredients:

2 med. carrots, diced
½ kielbasa sausage
1 onion, chopped
2 garlic cloves, chopped
2 celery stalks, chopped
2 cans tomatoes, cut up (16 oz. ea.)
2 c. sauerkraut
1 med. zucchini, cubed
2 cans dark red kidney beans, drained (15 oz. ea.)
1 can peas or frozen peas (15 oz.)
1 tsp. dried basil
½ tsp. ground sage
1 can tomato sauce (16 oz.)
   salt and pepper, to taste
   noodles (optional)

Directions:

1. In large pot, place carrots, sausage, onion, garlic, and celery; add a small amount of water.
2. Over medium heat, cook until almost tender.
3. Add tomatoes, sauerkraut, zucchini, beans, and peas; stir well.
4. Cook 2 hours, adding water if necessary.
5. Season with basil, sage, and salt and pepper, to taste.
6. Add noodles if desired; cook 20 minutes or until noodles are done.
7. Ladle into individual serving bowls.
8. Serve with crusty bread and salad.

Vegetable Soup

This is a delicious way to serve veggies at your meals. Add some crusty bread and a salad to make a complete meal.

Ingredients:

- 2 stalks celery, sliced
- 1 stalk fresh broccoli, chopped
- 3 carrots, sliced
- ½ c. burgundy wine
- ½ c. water
- 2 med. potatoes, cut into small chunks
- 12 fresh tomatoes, diced
- 2 med. onions, sliced
- 3 garlic cloves, crushed
- 1 eggplant, diced
- 2 med. small zucchini, in medium size chunks
- ¼ lb. mushrooms, sliced
- 3 Tbs. tomato paste
- 3 Tbs. molasses
- 1 tsp. dill weed
  salt and pepper, to taste
  butter, for sauté

Directions:

1. In large pot, over medium heat, add celery, broccoli, and carrots, wine, and enough water to cover; cook 20 minutes.
2. In large skillet melt butter; sauté onions, garlic, and potatoes; season with salt and pepper to taste. Add to soup pot.
3. Cook until vegetables are just about tender.
4. Reduce heat to low.
5. Add egg plant, zucchini, tomato paste, mushrooms, molasses, and dill weed; stir well.

6. Cover; simmer 20 minutes; adjust seasonings if necessary.
7. Serve hot; top with sour cream and fresh parsley.
8. Note: This soup is better reheated on the second day as flavors are enhanced.

Avocado Soup

This is an interesting soup that is served chilled. It is a nice addition to a very spicy meal because it cools down the action of the spices.

Ingredients:

¼ c. butter
¼ c. flour
2 avocados, 1 mashed, 1 cubed
1 qt. milk
¼ c. cream, whipped
¼ tsp. powdered ginger
1-2 tsp. minced preserved ginger (optional)
    rind of 1 orange
    salt, to taste

Directions:

1. In top of double boiler, melt butter; add flour and blend with wire whisk.
2. In small saucepan, bring milk to boil; add to butter and flour mixture, stirring vigorously with a whisk.
3. Add salt, ginger, and orange rind.
4. Cook while stirring, until the mixture has thickened.
5. Mash or sieve one avocado, and add to the sauce.
6. Stir in thoroughly; chill.
7. Serve in chilled soup bowls or cups.
8. Garnish with remaining avocado, whipped cream, and ginger.

Potato Mushroom Soup

This recipe is a real change of pace from the traditional potato soup. It is delicious served with crusty bread and salad for a complete meal.

Ingredients:

3 lg. potatoes, peeled, cubed
½ lb. fresh oyster and chanterelle mushrooms, sliced
6 c. cold water
2 garlic cloves, minced
1 bay leaf
2 Tbs. canola oil
1 Tbs. flour
1 shallot, minced
2 Tbs. tarragon vinegar
2 Tbs. chives, chopped
4 Tbs. sour cream
   sprig of fresh rosemary
   pinch of dried marjoram
   salt and pepper, to taste

Directions:

1. In medium stockpot, place potatoes, mushrooms, garlic, bay leaf, rosemary, marjoram, and salt and pepper, to taste; cover with 6 cups cold water.
2. Over medium heat, cook until it boils; reduce heat and cook 20 to 30 minutes.
3. In small saucepan, over medium-high heat, heat oil; when hot, sprinkle in flour and shallots. Brown while stirring constantly to make a roux.
4. Add some cooking liquid from soup to thin the roux; pour it into the soup.
5. Bring to gentle boil; remove from heat.
6. Add vinegar before serving.
7. Garnish with chives and sour cream.

Pumpkin Apple Soup

This recipe is very unique and can be served inside of a hollowed out pumpkin to make a tasty meal.

Ingredients:

    1 can pumpkin (28 oz.)
    1 can chicken broth or water (28 oz.)
    1 c. applesauce
    ¼ c. honey or maple syrup
    1 c. heavy cream
        salt and pepper, to taste
        cinnamon, to taste
        parsley, chopped
        sugared nuts, crushed
        small pumpkin for each serving, washed

Directions for soup:

1. In large saucepan, over medium heat, combine pumpkin, broth, and applesauce; heat through.
2. Add honey and salt and pepper, to taste.
3. Stir in cream just before serving.
4. Ladle soup into individual bowls or pumpkin bowls.
5. Garnish with cinnamon, parsley, and nuts.

Directions for pumpkin:

1. Cut top off each pumpkin and reserve.
2. Scoop out seeds and excess strings.
3. May use raw for soup; or rub pumpkins and caps with oil and bake just until tender.
4. Bake in a preheated oven at 325 degrees F. about 20 minutes for the mini pumpkins; about 30 to35 minutes for larger.
5. Cool; when ready to serve soup; fill almost full and replace cap at tilt.

Mushroom Bisque

Our family loves the taste of mushrooms and enjoys experimenting with the fresh and flavorful different types. This is a delicious soup and is very nourishing.

Ingredients:

2   lb. fresh mushrooms of your choice, washed
2   c. heavy cream
2   qt. chicken broth or vegetable broth for vegetarians
1½ med. onions, chopped
15 Tbs. butter
12 Tbs. flour
5   c. milk
4   Tbs. sherry (optional)
1   tsp. salt, or to taste
    white pepper
    hot red pepper sauce
    extra mushrooms, sliced, for garnish

Directions:

1. Cut dried ends off of mushroom stems.
2. Grind or chop remaining caps and stems very fine.
3. In large saucepan, add broth, onions, and chopped mushrooms; cover. Simmer 30 minutes.
4. In small skillet melt 1 tablespoon butter; sauté extra sliced mushrooms and reserve for garnish.
5. In small saucepan melt remaining butter; add flour and stir with wire whisk until blended.
6. In another small saucepan, bring milk to boil; add to butter-flour mixture, stirring vigorously with whisk until sauce is thickened and smooth; stir in cream.
7. Combine mushroom broth mixture with the sauce.
8. Season to taste with salt, pepper and pepper sauce.
9. Reheat and add sherry before serving.
10. Garnish with sautéed mushrooms.

Stilton Vegetable Soup

This is a wonderful vegetable soup and the flavor is really great with the addition of cheese and toasted nuts to top it off.

Ingredients:

1½ c. celery, finely chopped
1   lg. onion, finely chopped
1   lg. garlic clove, minced
1   c. water
1   bay leaf
½   tsp. dried thyme, crumbled
2   Tbs. butter, unsalted
2   baking potatoes, peeled, thinly sliced
2   c. chicken or vegetable broth
1   c. half and half cream
1½ c. Stilton cheese, crumbled
¼   c. sherry
3   Tbs. hazelnuts, toasted, chopped
    salt and pepper, to taste

Directions:

1. In large saucepan, over medium heat, add celery, onion, garlic, water, and bay leaf; cook 5 minutes.
2. Add thyme and butter; mix well.
3. Add potatoes to vegetables with broth; cover and simmer 15 minutes.
4. Discard bay leaf.
5. In blender or food processor, purée soup in batches.
6. Transfer back to covered pan; stir in cream.
7. Over low heat, reheat soup.
8. Add cheese and whisk until melted and soup is smooth.
9. Stir in sherry, salt and pepper to taste; do not let soup boil.
10. Ladle into individual serving bowls.
11. Garnish with hazelnuts.

Roasted Carrot Soup

The roasted veggies in this soup give it a delicious and unique flavor. Serve with some crusty bread and salad for a filling meal.

Ingredients for soup:

   1 c. yellow onion, diced
10 c. carrots, peeled, diced
   1 c. yellow onion, diced
   1 c. celery, diced
   1 Tbs. garlic, minced
   1 Tbs. ginger, peeled, chopped
   8 c. vegetable stock
   3 Tbs. oatmeal, rolled
   1 tsp. sea salt
 ¼ tsp. white pepper, ground
   1 tsp. nutmeg, ground
     chives, chopped
     cooking oil spray

Directions:

1. Preheat oven to 400 degrees F.
2. Lightly spray a roasting pan with cooking oil.
3. Place carrots in pan; bake 10 minutes stirring every 3 minutes.
4. Add onions, celery, garlic, and ginger to pan; mix well.
5. Return to oven; bake 5 minutes.
6. In large pot, over medium heat, add vegetables and vegetable stock.
7. Stir in oatmeal; bring contents to boil.
8. Reduce heat to low; simmer 10 to 15 minutes or until vegetables are soft and oats are cooked.
9. While simmering, stir in salt, pepper, and nutmeg.
10. Remove from heat; cool to lukewarm.

11. In blender or food processor, purée soup until smooth.
12. Reheat over low heat.
13. Ladle into bowls and garnish with chives.

Yields: 6 to 8 servings

Beer Cheese Soup

This soup is a bit unusual but makes a wonderful, tasty meal when served with some garlic bread and salad.

Ingredients:

2 Tbs. butter
1 sm. onion, chopped
1 med. stalk celery, thinly sliced
2 Tbs. flour
¼ tsp. pepper
¼ tsp. ground mustard
1 can or bottle of beer or nonalcoholic beer
1 c. milk
2 c. Cheddar cheese, shredded
  popped popcorn, if desired

Directions:

1. In 2-quart saucepan, over medium heat, melt butter.
2. Sauté onion and celery, 2 minutes, stirring occasionally, until tender.
3. Stir in flour, pepper, and mustard.
4. Add beer and milk; mix well.
5. Heat to boiling, boil 1 minute stirring constantly.
6. Reduce heat to low; gradually stir in cheese, stirring constantly, just until cheese is melted.
7. Ladle into individual serving bowls.
8. Sprinkle each serving with popcorn.

French Onion Soup

This is a delightful soup as a first course, light yet satisfying. If the flavor of the soup is not strong enough, just add more bouillon cubes to desired taste.

Ingredients:

   6 beef bouillon cubes
   6 c. water
   2 med. red onions, sliced
   3 lg. garlic cloves, minced
   ½ c. red wine
   1 tsp. black pepper
   3 c. croutons
   6 pieces of mozzarella cheese, thinly sliced
      fresh parsley, chopped

Directions:

   1. In large bowl, dissolve bouillon cubes in water.
   2. In large saucepan, add bouillon, onions, garlic, red wine, and pepper; cover.
   3. Over medium-high heat cook until onions become transparent, stirring occasionally.
   4. Reduce heat to simmer, and cook 20 to 25 minutes.
   5. Preheat oven to 500 degrees F. (broil)
   6. When ready to serve, pour soup ⅛-inch from top of heatproof bowl.
   7. Place croutons on top then a slice of cheese.
   8. Place bowl in oven; broil 2 to 3 minutes, or until cheese is melted.
   9. Note: Use caution as bowl will be very hot!
   10. Remove from oven.
   11. Place fresh parsley on top and serve with crusty bread and a salad.

Yields: 6 servings.

Egg Drop Soup

This soup is quick, easy, and a perfect beginning to a Chinese banquet, still being light enough to enjoy all of the other foods.

Ingredients:

   3 c. chicken broth
   1 tsp. salt
   2 Tbs. cold water
   1 Tbs. cornstarch
   1 egg, slightly beaten
   1 scallion and top, finely chopped

Directions:

1. Bring chicken broth to a boil in soup pot; add salt.
2. Stir a small amount of beaten egg at a time into the hot broth.
3. In small bowl, mix together cold water and cornstarch; add to broth.
4. Cook until clear and slightly thickened, stirring constantly.
5. Remove from heat and ladle into serving bowls.
6. Garnish with a sprinkle of chopped scallion.

Thai Chicken Soup

This is a favorite recipe for our family. You can delete the chicken and the fish sauce for a vegetarian soup.

Ingredients:

   ¼ c. fish sauce
   1 Tbs. red curry paste, less for milder soup
   2 cans coconut milk
   4 chicken breasts, cut up
   2 cans straw mushrooms
      small amount of lime juice or 2 lime leaves
      cashews
      cilantro

Directions:

1. In large saucepan, over medium heat, combine coconut milk, red curry paste, and chicken; cook 15 minutes.
2. Add mushrooms and cook 1 minute.
3. Stir in fish sauce then lime juice.
4. Ladle into individual soup bowls; sprinkle with cashews and cilantro.

Split Pea Soup

This is a wonderful soup to make for any occasion and especially during the long cold winter months. Try it with some thick crusty rolls or bread and a salad for a quick meal.

Ingredients:

1   lb. split green peas
7   c. water
2   c. potatoes, diced
1½ c. onions, chopped
1   c. celery, cubed
1   c. carrot, sliced
1   garlic clove, crushed
1   Tbs. salt
¼   tsp. pepper
¼   tsp. bottled red pepper sauce
1   pork hock, smoked (1½ lb.)

Directions:

1. Sort peas and rinse under cold running water; drain.
2. Place into a slow cooker; add potatoes, onions, celery, carrot, and seasonings, along with pork hock.
3. Cook 6 to 8 hours.
4. Remove pork hock from pot; cut meat from bone into small pieces; return to slow cooker.
5. Ladle soup into individual bowls.

Mother's Day Delights Cookbook
A Collection of Mother's Day Recipes
Cookbook Delights Holiday Series-Book 5

Wines and Spirits

Table of Contents

Page

About Cooking with Alcohol

Some recipes in this cookbook contain, among other ingredients, liquors. It is for the purpose of obtaining desired flavor and achieving culinary appreciation and not to be abused in any way. In cooking and baking, alcohol evaporates and only the flavor may be enjoyed. When mixed in cold, however, such as in desserts, caution must be exercised. These recipes are intended for people who may consume small amounts of alcohol in a responsible and safe manner.

I live in Washington State and we are proud of our wine production. Washington State is rapidly gaining prestige as a premier wine producer. Do enjoy the art of wine tasting and enjoy the completeness and uniqueness of each wine. It is an art to enjoy and savor in moderation.

If consumption of even small amounts of alcoholic ingredients presents a problem, in whatever form, please substitute coffee flavor syrups, found in coffee sections of supermarkets. For example, instead of Southern Comfort liqueur, substitute with Irish Cream or Amaretto Syrup.

Karen Jean Matsko Hood

Black Russian

Easy and refreshing! Enjoy with your company on this special occasion.

Ingredients:

> ¾ oz. coffee liqueur
> 1½ oz. vodka

Directions:

> 1. Pour ingredients over ice cubes in an old-fashioned glass.

Coconut Rum Blend

This makes a great rum blend.

Ingredients:

  1 oz. coconut rum
  ½ oz. amaretto
  4 oz. orange juice
  ½ oz. grenadine

Directions:

1. In shaker jar, combine all ingredients.
2. Add ice.
3. Serve.

Mango and Coconut Daiquiri

This is a delicious daiquiri.

Ingredients:

  1 c. mango, largely diced
  1 c. ice
  2 oz. white rum
  2 Tbs. fresh lime juice
  2 Tbs. coconut cream
  1 tsp. sugar
    coconut shavings, for garnish

Directions:

1. In blender, mix all ingredients except coconut shavings.
2. Blend until smooth.
3. Garnish with coconut shavings.
4. Pour into chilled glasses.

Eggnog Rum

This is a creamy and delicious drink for your next special occasion or holiday meal. A cooked egg custard is used to avoid any problems associated with uncooked eggs.

Ingredients for custard:

> 6 lg. eggs, slightly beaten
> ⅔ c. sugar
> ⅛ tsp salt, or to taste
> 5 c. milk
> 2 tsp. vanilla extract

Ingredients for eggnog:

> 2 c. heavy whipping cream, sweetened
> 4 Tbs. powdered sugar
> 1 tsp. vanilla extract
> 1 c. light rum
> ground nutmeg
> soft custard (recipe below)

Directions for custard:

1. In heavy 2-quart saucepan, mix eggs, sugar, and salt; gradually stir in milk.
2. Cook over medium heat, 10 to 15 minutes, stirring constantly, until mixture just coats a metal spoon.
3. Remove from heat; stir in vanilla.
4. Place saucepan in cold water until custard is cool.
5. Cover; refrigerate 2 hours but no longer than 24 hours before adding to eggnog mixture above.

Directions for eggnog:

1. Just before serving, combine sweetened whipping cream, powdered sugar, and vanilla in a chilled medium bowl.

2. Beat with electric mixer on high speed until stiff.
3. Gently stir 2 cups of the sweetened whipped cream and rum into custard.
4. Pour custard mixture into small punch bowl.
5. Drop remaining sweetened whipped cream in mounds onto custard mixture.
6. Sprinkle with nutmeg.

Vodka Sipper

This makes a creamy and delicious drink to share with company on this special day.

Ingredients:

1½ c. fresh raspberries
1½ c. unsweetened white grape juice
1½ c. raspberry sherbet
¼ c. water
2 Tbs. lemon juice
vodka
ice cubes

Directions:

1. In blender container, combine raspberries and grape juice; cover and process until smooth.
2. Strain mixture through several layers of dampened cheesecloth, reserving liquid.
3. In blender container combine reserved liquid, sherbet, water, and lemon juice; cover and process until smooth.
4. Pour mixture over ice cubes in tall chilled glasses.
5. Slowly add 2 ounces of vodka over the ice cubes in each drink, without stirring.
6. Serve with a straw and a few raspberries for garnish.

White Russian

This white Russian is a creamy, light and soothing drink to share with company for a special occasion.

Ingredients:

> 1½ oz. vodka
> ¾ oz. coffee-flavored liqueur
> ¾ oz. light cream or milk
> ice

Directions:

1. In shaker jar, mix vodka and liqueur together.
2. Pour into glass over ice.
3. Carefully float the cream on top to serve.

Yellow Rattler

The orange juice adds a refreshing flavor to the gin and vermouth.

Ingredients:

> 1 oz. gin
> ½ oz. sweet vermouth
> ½ oz. dry vermouth
> 1 Tbs. orange juice
> 1 cocktail onion

Directions:

1. In shaker jar combine gin, vermouths, and orange juice with ice; shake well.
2. Strain into chilled cocktail glass.
3. Add cocktail onion and serve.

Coconut Canal

Try this coconut cocktail.

Ingredients:

¼ can of condensed milk
2 coconuts and all water
1 Tbs. gin
1 tsp. aromatic bitters

Directions:

1. Mix coconut water and jelly with condensed milk.
2. Add gin and bitters.
3. Chill slightly.
4. Serve with cracked ice.

Coconut Grove Drink

Coconut rum provides a nice flavor combination for this tropical drink.

Ingredients:

1½ oz. coconut rum
1 oz. Crème de Bananes
1 oz. white rum
4 oz. pineapple juice
1 tsp. lemon juice

Directions:

1. Mix all ingredients together.
2. Shake and strain into ice-filled glass.
3. Garnish with pineapple and lemon slices.

Wine Cooler

This is a refreshing wine cooler to serve to your guests at a special occasion dinner.

Ingredients:

½ oz. grapefruit juice
½ oz. pineapple juice
½ oz. lime juice
½ oz. lemon juice
4 oz. Chablis white wine
6 oz. lime soda
  crushed ice

Directions:

1. In shaker jar combine lemon, grapefruit, pineapple, lime, and lemon juice together.
2. Add ice and shake well to blend juices.
3. Pour into a tall, chilled wine glass; add lime soda.
4. Pour the iced juices in, swirl and serve.

Avocado Daiquiri

This is an unusual but delicious drink to serve at your special occasion.

Ingredients:

1 c. ice
1½ oz. light rum
¾ oz. fresh lime juice
¼ med. avocado
1 lime wedge

Directions:

1. Crush ice in blender; add rum, lime juice, and avocado; blend until smooth.
2. Pour into chilled glasses; garnish with lime wedge.

Chocolate Black Russian

This is a delicious creamy alternative to the traditional black or white Russian with the added chocolate.

Ingredients:

1 oz. coffee flavored liqueur
½ oz. vodka
5 oz. chocolate ice cream

Directions:

1. In blender container combine all ingredients.
2. On low speed, process for 1 minute.
3. Pour into a chilled champagne flute and serve.

White Zin Raspberry Cooler

On a sunny day what could be any more delicious and cool than this wonderful drink to serve and sip out on the deck with company.

Ingredients:

4 oz. white Zinfandel
1 oz. raspberry daiquiri mix
2½ oz. lemon lime soda
1 tsp. sugar
½ oz. grenadine

Directions:

1. In shaker jar place Zinfandel, raspberry mix, lemon lime soda, and sugar; shake well.
2. Pour into chilled, tall glasses over ice.
3. Pour grenadine over the ice.

Vodka Blueberry Liqueur

This spirit takes some waiting time, but if you make it during blueberry season, you can enjoy the taste of fresh blueberries year round!

Ingredients:

> 1 c. sugar
> 2 c. vodka
> 3 c. fresh blueberries, washed, crushed lightly

Directions:

1. In a half-gallon jar, dissolve sugar in vodka.
2. Pour in blueberries and cover the jar.
3. Store in a cool, dark place or the refrigerator, for 2 months.
4. Occasionally shake gently to blend ingredients.
5. Strain; serve in chilled cordial glasses or over ice.

Hot Buttered Rum

This is a delicious drink to share with your guests on a chilly day or cool evening.

Ingredients:

> 2 c. apple cider
> 1 cinnamon stick
> 1 tsp. brown sugar
> 1 Tbs. lemon juice
> 2 Tbs. honey
> 2 Tbs. butter, unsalted, cold
> 2 Tbs. rum, or to taste
> 2 cinnamon sticks, for stirring
> ground nutmeg, for garnish

Directions:

1. In small saucepan, over medium heat, add cider, cinnamon stick, sugar, lemon, and honey.
2. Bring mixture slowly to a boil.
3. Reduce heat to low; simmer 2 minutes.
4. Pour 1 tablespoon rum in each of 2 mugs.
5. Discard cinnamon stick and pour in cider mixture.
6. Top each drink with 1 tablespoon cold butter and a sprinkle of nutmeg.
7. Serve immediately, with a new cinnamon stick in each mug, for stirring.

Yields: 2 servings.

Vaina

This cocktail was originally created for Chilean soldiers during the Pacific War in the nineteenth century, and now you can enjoy it with friends.

Ingredients:

    2 oz. sherry
    1 oz. chocolate liqueur
    1 oz. cognac or brandy
    3 Tbs. powdered sugar
    1 egg yolk
      ice
      ground cinnamon

Directions:

1. In shaker jar, combine sherry, chocolate liqueur, cognac, sugar, and egg yolk with ice; shake well.
2. Serve in a chilled wine glass.
3. Add a dash of ground cinnamon to the top.

Vodka Lime and Soda

This makes an easy and refreshing drink to enjoy with your guests on this special occasion.

Ingredients:

1½ oz. vodka
1½ oz. lime cordial, or lime juice sweetened to taste
5   oz. carbonated soda
     crushed ice

Directions:

1. In shaker jar combine vodka and lime cordial; blend well.
2. Pour over ice and add soda; stir and serve.

Cherry Cider

Add some romantic, spiced cherry apple cider to your Mother's Day dinner. Spiced cider is always a delicious drink.

Ingredients:

2 qt. apple cider
2 c. sweet cherry juice
1 pc. cinnamon stick (3-inch)

Directions:

1. In medium saucepan combine cider, cherry juice, and cinnamon stick; bring to boil.
2. Reduce heat and simmer 15 minutes.
3. Pour into warm mugs and serve.

Yields: 8 to 10 servings.

Amaretto

This recipe makes a delicious amaretto, so close; it is hard to tell it from the real thing.

Ingredients:

- 1 c. water
- 1 c. white sugar
- ½ c. brown sugar
- 2 c. vodka
- 2 Tbs. almond extract
- 2 tsp. vanilla extract

Directions:

1. In small saucepan, over medium heat, combine water and sugars.
2. Heat until boiling, and sugar is dissolved.
3. Remove from heat; cool 10 minutes.
4. Stir vodka, almond extract, and vanilla extract into the mixture.
5. Store in a sealed bottle.

Coconut Loco

This makes a pleasing mixed drink. Enjoy!

Ingredients:

- 1 can cream of coconut
- 8 oz. **each:** grenadine, tequila, vodka, gin, rum crushed ice

Directions:

1. In blender, add all ingredients with crushed ice.
2. Pour into chilled glasses and serve.

Strawberry Shortcake Drink

This is a creamy strawberry drink that makes a refreshing dessert drink.

Ingredients:

  1 part strawberry schnapps
  1 part sparkling lemon lime soda
  1 Tbs. grenadine
  1 c. cream

Directions:

  1. In a tall, cold glass, add schnapps and soda.
  2. Add grenadine; stir gently.
  3. Top with cream.

Strawberry Blonde

Strawberry liqueur combines with golden ginger ale for a refreshing, thirst quenching drink.

Ingredients:

  1 oz. strawberry liqueur
  1 tsp. sugar
  1 strawberry, whole
    ginger ale

Directions:

  1. Put a thin rim of sugar around a chilled cocktail glass.
  2. Put crushed ice into glass; pour liqueur over ice; add ginger ale to fill.
  3. Add strawberry for decoration.
  4. Note: If you would like a non-alcoholic drink, substitute the liqueur for strawberry syrup.

Festival Information

Mother's Day Dates Around the World

Mother's Day is always celebrated each year on the same day in each country. The date changes each year based on which date that specific day falls on.

Country	Day
India	Second Sunday in the month of May
United States	Second Sunday in the month of May
Australia	Second Sunday in the month of May
Belgium	Second Sunday in the month of May
Brazil	Second Sunday in the month of May
Canada	Second Sunday in the month of May
Denmark	Second Sunday in the month of May
Finland	Second Sunday in the month of May
Germany	Second Sunday in the month of May
Greece	Second Sunday in the month of May
Italy	Second Sunday in the month of May
Japan	Second Sunday in the month of May
Turkey	Second Sunday in the month of May
Sweden	Last Sunday in the month of May
Austria	First Sunday in the month of May
Hong Kong	First Sunday in the month of May
Italy	First Sunday in the month of May
Netherlands	First Sunday in the month of May
New Zealand	First Sunday in the month of May
Taiwan	First Sunday in the month of May
Hungary	First Sunday in the month of May
Portugal	First Sunday in the month of May
South Africa	First Sunday in the month of May
Spain	First Sunday in the month of May
South Amer.	Second Wednesday in the month of May
Mexico	Second Wednesday in the month of May
Bahrain	Second Wednesday in the month of May
Malaysia	Second Wednesday in the month of May

Oman	Second Wednesday in the month of May
Pakistan	Second Wednesday in the month of May
Qatar	Second Wednesday in the month of May
Saudi Arabia	Second Wednesday in the month of May
Singapore	Second Wednesday in the month of May
United Arab Emirates	Second Wednesday in the month of May
Norway	Second Sunday in the month of February

Mother's Day is celebrated in practically every country, and in every city and state. There usually are not any specific fairs or festivals for this particular day, so most everyone has their own particular way of celebrating this special day with the "mom" in their life.

We recommend that you check with your local area chamber of commerce for any specific events in your particular area, and hope you and the "mom" in your life are able to share this special time together.

U.S. and Metric Measurement Charts

Here are some measurement equivalents to help you with exchanges. There was a time when many people thought the entire world would convert to the metric scale. While most of the world has, America still has not. Metric conversions in cooking are vitally important to preparing a tasty recipe. Here are simple conversion tables that should come in handy.

U.S. Measurement Equivalents

a few grains/pinch/dash (dry) =
less than $\frac{1}{8}$ teaspoon
a dash (liquid) = a few drops
3 teaspoons = 1 tablespoon
$\frac{1}{2}$ tablespoon = $1\frac{1}{2}$ teaspoons
1 tablespoon = 3 teaspoons
2 tablespoons = 1 fluid ounce
4 tablespoons = $\frac{1}{4}$ cup
$5\frac{1}{3}$ tablespoons = $\frac{1}{3}$ cup
8 tablespoons = $\frac{1}{2}$ cup
8 tablespoons = 4 fluid ounces
$10\frac{2}{3}$ tablespoons = $\frac{2}{3}$ cup
12 tablespoons = $\frac{3}{4}$ cup
16 tablespoons = 1 cup
16 tablespoons = 8 fluid ounces
$\frac{1}{8}$ cup = 2 tablespoons
$\frac{1}{4}$ cup = 4 tablespoons
$\frac{1}{4}$ cup = 2 fluid ounces
$\frac{1}{3}$ cup = 5 tablespoons plus 1 teaspoon
$\frac{1}{2}$ cup = 8 tablespoons
1 cup = 16 tablespoons
1 cup = 8 fluid ounces
1 cup = $\frac{1}{2}$ pint
2 cups = 1 pint
2 pints = 1 quart
4 quarts (liquid) = 1 gallon
8 quarts (dry) = 1 peck
4 pecks (dry) = 1 bushel
1 kilogram = approximately 2 pounds
1 liter=approximately 4 cups or 1quart

Approximate Metric Equivalents by Volume

U.S.	Metric
$\frac{1}{4}$ cup	= 60 milliliters
$\frac{1}{2}$ cup	= 120 milliliters
1 cup	= 230 milliliters
$1\frac{1}{4}$ cups	= 300 milliliters
$1\frac{1}{2}$ cups	= 360 milliliters
2 cups	= 460 milliliters
$2\frac{1}{2}$ cups	= 600 milliliters
3 cups	= 700 milliliters
4 cups (1 quart)	= .95 liter
1.06 quarts	= 1 liter
4 quarts (1 gallon)	= 3.8 liters

Approximate Metric Equivalents by Weight

U.S.	Metric
$\frac{1}{4}$ ounce	= 7 grams
$\frac{1}{2}$ ounce	= 14 grams
1 ounce	= 28 grams
$1\frac{1}{4}$ ounces	= 35 grams
$1\frac{1}{2}$ ounces	= 40 grams
$2\frac{1}{2}$ ounces	= 70 grams
4 ounces	= 112 grams
5 ounces	= 140 grams
8 ounces	= 228 grams
10 ounces	= 280 grams
15 ounces	= 425 grams
16 ounces (1 pound)	= 454 grams

Glossary

Aerate: A synonym for sift; to pass ingredients through a fine-mesh device to break up large pieces and incorporate air into ingredients to make them lighter.

Al dente: "To the tooth," in Italian. The pasta is cooked just enough to maintain a firm, chewy texture.

Baste: To brush or spoon liquid fat or juices over meat during roasting to add flavor and prevent drying out.

Bias-slice: To slice a food crosswise at a 45-degree angle.

Bind: To thicken a sauce or hot liquid by stirring in ingredients such as eggs, flour, butter, or cream until it holds together.

Blackened: Popular Cajun-style cooking method. Seasoned foods are cooked over high heat in a super-heated heavy skillet until charred.

Blanch: To scald, as in vegetables being prepared for freezing; as in almonds so as to remove skins.

Blend: To mix or fold two or more ingredients together to obtain equal distribution throughout the mixture.

Braise: To brown meat in oil or other fat and then cook slowly in liquid. The effect of braising is to tenderize the meat.

Bread: To coat food with crumbs (usually with soft or dry bread crumbs), sometimes seasoned.

Brown: To quickly sauté, broil, or grill either at the beginning or at the end of meal preparation, often to enhance flavor, texture, or eye appeal.

Brush: To use a pastry brush to coat a food such as meat or pastry with melted butter, glaze, or other liquid.

Butterfly: To cut open a food such as pork chops down the center without cutting all the way through, and then spread apart.

Caramelization: Browning sugar over a flame, with or without the addition of some water to aid the process. The temperature range in which sugar caramelizes is approximately 320 to 360 degrees F.

Clarify: To remove impurities from butter or stock by heating the liquid, then straining or skimming it.

Coddle: A cooking method in which foods (such as eggs) are put in separate containers and placed in a pan of simmering water for slow, gentle cooking.

Confit: To slowly cook pieces of meat in their own gently rendered fat.

Core: To remove the inedible center of fruits such as pineapples.

Cream: To beat vegetable shortening, butter, or margarine, with or without sugar, until light and fluffy. This process traps in air bubbles, later used to create height in cookies and cakes.

Crimp: To create a decorative edge on a pie crust. On a double pie crust, this also seals the edges together.

Curd: A custard-like pie or tart filling flavored with juice and zest of citrus fruit, usually lemon, although lime and orange may also be used.

Curdle: To cause semisolid pieces of coagulated protein to develop in food, usually as a result of the addition of an acid substance, or the overheating of milk or egg-based sauces.

Custard: A mixture of beaten egg, milk, and possibly other ingredients such as sweet or savory flavorings, which are cooked with gentle heat, often in a water bath or double boiler. As pie filling, the custard is frequently cooked and chilled before being layered into a baked crust.

Deglaze: To add liquid to a pan in which foods have been fried or roasted, in order to dissolve the caramelized juices stuck to the bottom of the pan.

Dot: To sprinkle food with small bits of an ingredient such as butter to allow for even melting.

Dredge: To sprinkle lightly and evenly with sugar or flour. A dredger has holes pierced on the lid to sprinkle evenly.

Drippings: The liquids left in the bottom of a roasting or frying pan after meat is cooked. Drippings are generally used for gravies and sauces.

Drizzle: To pour a liquid such as a sweet glaze or melted butter in a slow, light trickle over food.

Dust: To sprinkle food lightly with spices, sugar, or flour for a light coating.

Egg Wash: A mixture of beaten eggs (yolks, whites, or whole eggs) with either milk or water. Used to coat cookies and other baked goods to give them a shine when baked.

Emulsion: A mixture of liquids, one being a fat or oil and the other being water based so that tiny globules of one are suspended in the other. This may involve the use of stabilizers, such as egg or custard. Emulsions may be temporary or permanent.

Entrée: A French term that originally referred to the first course of a meal, served after the soup and before the meat courses. In the United States, it refers to the main dish of a meal.

Fillet: To remove the bones from meat or fish for cooking.

Filter: To remove lumps, excess liquid, or impurities by passing through paper or cheesecloth.

Firm-Ball Stage: In candy making, the point at which boiling syrup dropped in cold water forms a ball that is compact yet gives slightly to the touch.

Flambé: To ignite a sauce or other liquid so that it flames.

Flan: An open pie filled with sweet or savory ingredients; also, a Spanish dessert of baked custard covered with caramel.

Flute: To create a decorative scalloped or undulating edge on a pie crust or other pastry.

Fricassee: Usually a stew in which the meat is cut up, lightly cooked in butter, and then simmered in liquid until done.

Frizzle: To cook thin slices of meat in hot oil until crisp and slightly curly.

Ganache: A rich chocolate filling or coating made with chocolate, vegetable shortening, and possibly heavy cream. It can coat cakes or cookies, and be used as a filling for truffles.

Glaze: A liquid that gives an item a shiny surface. Examples are fruit jams that have been heated or chocolate thinned with melted vegetable shortening. Also, to cover a food with such a liquid.

Gratin: To bind together or combine food with a liquid such as cream, milk, béchamel sauce, or tomato sauce, in a shallow dish. The mixture is then baked until cooked and set.

Hard-Ball Stage: In candy making, the point at which syrup has cooked long enough to form a solid ball in cold water.

Hull (also husk): To remove the leafy parts of soft fruits, such as strawberries or blackberries.

Infusion: To extract flavors by soaking them in liquid heated in a covered pan. The term also refers to the liquid resulting from this process.

Jerk or Jamaican Jerk Seasoning: A dry mixture of various spices such as chilies, thyme, garlic, onions, and cinnamon or cloves used to season meats such as chicken or pork.

Julienne: To cut into long, thin strips.

Jus: The natural juices released by roasting meats.

Larding: To inset strips of fat into pieces of meat, so that the braised meat stays moist and juicy.

Marble: To gently swirl one food into another.

Marinate: To combine food with aromatic ingredients to add flavor.

Meringue: Egg whites beaten until they are stiff, then sweetened. It can be used as the topping for pies or baked as cookies.

Mull: To slowly heat cider with spices and sugar.

Parboil: To partly cook in a boiling liquid.

Peaks: The mounds made in a mixture. For example, egg white that has been whipped to stiffness. Peaks are "stiff" if they stay upright or "soft" if they curl over.

Pesto: A sauce usually made of fresh basil, garlic, olive oil, pine nuts, and cheese. The ingredients are finely chopped and then mixed, uncooked, with pasta. Generally, the term refers to any uncooked sauce made of finely chopped herbs and nuts.

Pipe: To force a semisoft food through a bag (either a pastry bag or a plastic bag with one corner cut off) to decorate food.

Pressure Cooking: To cook using steam trapped under a locked lid to produce high temperatures and achieve fast cooking time.

Purée: To mash or sieve food into a thick liquid.

Ramekin: A small baking dish used for individual servings of sweet and savory dishes.

Reduce: To cook liquids down so that some of the water evaporates.

Refresh: To pour cold water over freshly cooked vegetables to prevent further cooking and to retain color.

Roux: A cooked paste usually made from flour and butter used to thicken sauces.

Sauté: To cook foods quickly in a small amount of oil in a skillet or sauté pan over direct heat.

Scald: To heat a liquid, usually a dairy product, until it almost boils.

Sear: To seal in a meat's juices by cooking it quickly using very high heat.

Seize: To form a thick, lumpy mass when melted (usually applies to chocolate).

Sift: To remove large lumps from a dry ingredient such as flour or confectioners' sugar by passing it through a fine mesh. This process also incorporates air into the ingredients, making them lighter.

Simmer: To cook food in a liquid at a low enough temperature that small bubbles begin to break the surface.

Steam: To cook over boiling water in a covered pan. This method keeps foods' shape, texture, and nutritional value intact better than methods such as boiling.

Steep: To soak dry ingredients (tea leaves, ground coffee, herbs, spices, etc.) in liquid until the flavor is infused into the liquid.

Stewing: To brown small pieces of meat, poultry, or fish, then simmer them with vegetables or other ingredients in enough liquid to cover them, usually in a closed pot on the stove, in the oven, or with a slow cooker.

Thin: To reduce a mixture's thickness with the addition of more liquid.

Truss: To use string, skewers, or pins to hold together a food to maintain its shape while it cooks (usually applied to meat or poultry).

Unleavened: Baked goods that contain no agents to give them volume, such as baking powder, baking soda, or yeast.

Vinaigrette: A general term referring to any sauce made with vinegar, oil, and seasonings.

Zest: The thin, brightly colored outer part of the rind of citrus fruits. It contains volatile oils, used as a flavoring.

Recipe Index of Mother's Day Delights

315

Reader Feedback Form

Dear Reader,

We are very interested in what our readers think. Please fill in the form below and return it to:

Whispering Pine Press International, Inc.
c/o Mothers Day Delights Cookbook
P.O. Box 214, Spokane Valley, WA 99037-0214 USA
Phone: (509) 928-8700 | Fax: (509) 922-9949
Email: sales@WhisperingPinePress.com
Publisher Website: www.WhisperingPinePress.com
Book Website: www.MothersDayDelights.net

Name: _____

Address: _____

City, St., Zip: _____

Phone/Fax: (____) _____ / (____) _____

Email: _____

Comments/Suggestions: _____

_____

_____

_____

_____

A great deal of care and attention has been exercised in the creation of this book. Designing a great cookbook that is original, fun, and easy to use has been a job that required many hours of diligence, creativity, and research. Although we strive to make this book completely error free, errors and discrepancies may not be completely excluded. If you come across any errors or discrepancies, please make a note of them and send them to our publishing office. We are constantly updating our manuscripts, eliminating errors, and improving quality.

Please contact us at the address above.

About the Cookbook Delights Series

The *Cookbook Delights Series* includes many different topics and themes. If you have a passion for food and wish to know more information about different foods, then this series of cookbooks will be beneficial to you. Each book features a different type of food, such as avocados, strawberries, huckleberries, salmon, vegetarian, lentils, almonds, cherries, coconuts, lemons, and many, many more.

The *Cookbook Delights Series* not only includes cookbooks about individual foods but also includes several holiday-themed cookbooks. Whatever your favorite holiday may be, chances are we have a cookbook with recipes designed with that holiday in mind. Some examples include *Halloween Delights, Thanksgiving Delights, Christmas Delights, Valentine Delights, Mother's Day Delights, St. Patrick's Day Delights,* and *Easter Delights.*

Each cookbook is designed for easy use and is organized into alphabetical sections. Over 250 recipes are included along with other interesting facts, folklore, and history of the featured food or theme. Each book comes with a beautiful full-color cover, ordering information, and a list of other upcoming books in the series.

Note cards, bookmarks, and a daily journal have been printed and are available to go along with each cookbook. You may view the entire line of cookbooks, journals, cards, posters, puzzles, and bookmarks by visiting our website at and www.mothersdaydelights.net, or you can email us with your questions and your comments to: sales@whisperingpinepress.com.

Please ask your local bookstore to carry these sets of books.

To order, please contact:

Whispering Pine Press International, Inc.
c/o Mothers Day Delights Cookbook
P.O. Box 214, Spokane Valley, WA 99037-0214 USA
Phone: (509) 9928-8700| Fax: (509) 922-9949
Email: sales@WhisperingPinePress.com
Publisher Website: www.WhisperingPinePress.com
Book Website: www.MothersDayDelights.net
SAN 253-200X

We Invite You to Join the Whispering Pine Press International, Inc., Book Club!

Whispering Pine Press International, Inc.
c/o Mothers Day Delights Cookbook
P.O. Box 214, Spokane Valley, WA 99037-0214 USA
Phone: (509) 928-8700l Fax: (509) 922-9949
Email: sales@WhisperingPinePress.com
Publisher Website: www.WhisperingPinePress.com
Book Website: www.MothersDayDelights.net

Buy 11 books and get the next one free, based on the average price of the first eleven purchased.

How the club works:
Simply use the order form below and order books from our catalog. You can buy just one at a time or all eleven at once. After the first eleven books are purchased, the next one is free. Please add shipping and handling as listed on this form. There are no purchase requirements at any time during your membership. Free book credit is based on the average price of the first eleven books purchased.

Join today! Pick your books and mail in the form today!
Yes! I want to join the Whispering Pine Press International, Inc., Book Club! Enroll me and send the books indicated below.

Title   Price
1. _____
2. _____
3. _____
4. _____
5. _____
6. _____
7. _____
8. _____
9. _____
10. _____
11. _____
Free Book Title: _____
Free Book Price: _____ Avg. Price: _____ Total Price: _____
Credit for the free book is based on the average price of the first 11 books purchased.
(Circle one) Check | Visa | MasterCard | Discover | American Express
Credit Card #: _____ Expiration Date: _____
Name: _____
Address: _____
City: _____ State: _____ Country: _____
Zip/Postal: _____ Phone: (_____)_____
Email: _____
Signature_____

Whispering Pine Press International, Inc. Fundraising Opportunities

Fundraising cookbooks are proven moneymakers and great keepsake providers for your group. Whispering Pine Press International, Inc., offers a very special personalized cookbook fundraising program that encourages success to organizations all across the USA.

Our prices are competitive and fair. Currently, we offer a special of 100 books with many free features and excellent customer service. Any purchase you make is guaranteed first-rate.

Flexibility is not a problem. If you have special needs, we guarantee our cooperation in meeting each of them. Our goal is to create a cookbook that goes beyond your expectations. We have the confidence and a record that promises continual success.

Another great fundraising program is the *Cookbook Delights Series* Program. With cookbook orders of 50 copies or more, your organization receives a huge discount, making for a prompt and lucrative solution.

We also specialize in assisting group fundraising – Christian, community, nonprofit, and academic among them. If you are struggling for a new idea, something that will enhance your success and broaden your appeal, Whispering Pine Press International, Inc., can help.

For more information, write, phone, or fax to:

Whispering Pine Press International, Inc.
P.O. Box 214, Spokane Valley, WA 99037-0214 USA
Phone: (509) 928-8700 | Fax: (509) 922-9949
Email: sales@WhisperingPinePress.com
Publisher Website: www.WhisperingPinePress.com
Book Website: www.MothersDayDelights.net
SAN 253-200X

Personalized and/or Translated Order Form for Any Book by Whispering Pine Press International, Inc.

Dear Readers:

If you or your organization wishes to have this book or any other of our books personalized, we will gladly accommodate your needs. For instance, if you would like to change the names of the characters in a book to the names of the children in your family or Sunday school class, we would be happy to work with you on such a project. We can add more information of your choosing and customize this book especially for your family, group, or organization.

We are also offering an option of translating your book into another language. Please fill out the form below telling us exactly how you would like us to personalize your book.

Please send your request to:

Whispering Pine Press International, Inc.
P.O. Box 214, Spokane Valley, WA 99037-0214 USA
Phone: (509) 928-8700 | Fax: (509) 922-9949
Email: sales@WhisperingPinePress.com
Publisher Website: www.WhisperingPinePress.com
Book Website: www.MothersDayDelights.net

Person/Organization placing request: _____

Date_____ Phone: (___) _____

Address_____ Fax: (___) _____

City_____ State_____ Zip: _____

Language of the book: _____

Please explain your request in detail: _____

_____

_____

_____

_____

_____

Mother's Day Delights Cookbook
A Collection of Mother's Day Recipes
How to Order

Get your additional copies of this book by returning an order form and your check, money order, or credit card information to:

Whispering Pine Press International, Inc.
P.O. Box 214, Spokane Valley, WA 99037-0214 USA
Phone: (509) 928-8700 | Fax: (509) 922-9949
Email: sales@WhisperingPinePress.com
Publisher Website: www.WhisperingPinePress.com
Book Website: www.OnionDelightsCookbook.com

Customer Name: _____

Address: _____

City, St., Zip: _____

Phone/Fax: _____

Email: _____

- -

Please send me _____ copies of _____

_____ at $_____

per copy and $4.95 for shipping and handling per book, plus

$2.95 each for additional books. Enclosed is my check, money

order, or charge my account for $_____.

☐ Check   ☐ Money Order   ☐ Credit Card

(*Circle One*) MasterCard | Discover | Visa | American Express

☐☐☐☐   ☐☐☐☐   ☐☐☐☐   ☐☐☐☐

Expiration Date: _____

_____
Signature

_____
Print Name

Whispering Pine Press International, Inc. Order Form
Gift-wrapping, Autographing, and Inscription
We are proud to offer personal autographing by the author. For a limited time this service is absolutely free!
Gift-wrapping is also available for $4.95 per item.

1. Sold To

Name: _____

Street/Route: _____

_____

City: _____

State: _____ Zip: _____

Country: _____

Gift message: _____

_____

Email address: _____

Daytime Phone: (___) ___-____

*Necessary for verifying orders

Home Phone: (___) ___-____

Fax: (___) ___-____

2. Ship To

☐ Is this a new or corrected address?

☐ Alternative Shipping Address

☐ Mailing Address

Name: _____

Address: _____

_____

City: _____

State: _____ Zip: _____

Country: _____

Email address: _____

3. Items Ordered

ISBN # /Item #	Size	Color	Qty.	Title or Description	Price	Total

4. Method Of Payment

International, Inc. (No Cash or COD's)

☐ Visa ☐ MasterCard ☐ Discover ☐ American Express ☐ Check/Money Order

Please make it payable to Whispering Pine Press International, Inc. (No Cash or COD's)

Account Number

Expiration Date

____ / ____

Month Year

☐☐☐ ☐☐☐ ☐☐☐ ☐☐

Signature_____

Cardholder's signature

Printed Name_____

Please print name of cardholder

Address of Cardholder_____

Subtotal	
Gift wrap $4.95 Each	
For delivery in WA add 8.7% sales tax.	
Shipping See chart at left	
6. Total	

5. Shipping & Handling

Continental US

US Postal Ground: For books please add $4.95 for the first book and $2.95 each for additional books.

All non-book items, add 15% of the Subtotal.

Please allow 1-4 weeks for delivery.

US Postal Air: Please add $15.00 shipping and handling.

Please allow 1-3 days for delivery.

Alaska, Hawaii, and the US Territories By Ship:

Please add 10% shipping and handling (minimum charge $15.00).

Please

By Air: Please add 12% shipping and handling (minimum charge $15.00).

Please allow 2 –6 weeks for delivery.

International By Ship: Please add 10% shipping and handling (minimum charge $15.00).

Please allow 6-12 weeks for delivery.

By Air: Please add 12% shipping and handling (minimum charge $15.00).

Please allow 2-6 weeks for delivery.

FedEx Shipments: Add $5.00 to the above airmail charges for overnight delivery.

Shop Online:
www.whisperingpinepress.com
Fax orders to: (509) 922-9949

Whispering Pine Press International, Inc.
P.O. Box 214
Spokane Valley, WA 99037-0214 USA
Phone: (509) 928-8700 • Fax: (509) 922-9949
Email: sales@whisperingpinepress.com
Website: www.whisperingpinepress.com

About the Author and Cook

Karen Jean Matsko Hood has always enjoyed cooking, baking, and experimenting with recipes. At this time Hood is working to complete a series of cookbooks that blends her skills and experience in cooking and entertaining. Hood entertains large groups of people and especially enjoys designing creative menus with holiday, international, ethnic, and regional themes.

Hood is publishing a cookbook series entitled the *Cookbook Delights Series,* in which each cookbook emphasizes a different food ingredient or theme. The first cookbook in the series is *Apple Delights Cookbook.* Hood is working to complete another series of cookbooks titled *Hood and Matsko Family Cookbooks,* which includes many recipes handed down from her family heritage and others that have emerged from more current family traditions. She has been invited to speak on talk radio shows on various topics, and favorite recipes from her cookbooks have been prepared on local television programs.

Hood was born and raised in Great Falls, Montana. As an undergraduate, she attended the College of St. Benedict in St. Joseph, Minnesota, and St. John's University in Collegeville, Minnesota. She attended the University of Great Falls in Great Falls, Montana. Hood received a B.S. Degree in Natural Science from the College of St. Benedict and minored in both Psychology and Secondary Education. Upon her graduation, Hood and her husband taught science and math on the island of St. Croix in the U.S. Virgin Islands. Hood has completed postgraduate classes at the University of Iowa in Iowa City, Iowa. In May 2001, she completed her Master's Degree in Pastoral Ministry at Gonzaga University in Spokane, Washington. She has taken postgraduate classes at Lewis and Clark College on the North Idaho college campus in Coeur d'Alene, Idaho, Taylor University in Fort Wayne, Indiana, Spokane Falls Community College, Spokane Community College, Washington State University, University of Washington, and Eastern Washington University. Hood is working on research projects to complete her Ph.D. in Leadership Studies at Gonzaga University in Spokane, Washington.

Hood resides in Greenacres, Washington, along with her husband, many of her sixteen children, and foster children. Her interests include writing, research, and teaching. She previously has volunteered as a court advocate in the Spokane juvenile court system for abused and neglected children. Hood is a literary advocate for youth and adults. Her hobbies include cooking, baking, collecting, photography, indoor and outdoor gardening, farming, and the cultivation of unusual flowering plants and orchids. She enjoys raising several specialty breeds of animals including Babydoll Southdown, Friesen, and Icelandic sheep, Icelandic horses, bichons frisés, cockapoos, Icelandic sheepdogs, a Newfoundland, a Rottweiler, a variety of Nubian and fainting goats, and a few rescue cats. Hood also enjoys bird-watching and finds all aspects of nature precious.

She demonstrates a passionate appreciation of the environment and a respect for all life. She also invites you to visit her websites:

www.KarenJeanMatskoHood.com
www.KarenJeanMatskoHoodBookstore.com
www.KarenJeanMatskoHoodBlog.com
www.KarensKidsBooks.com
www.KarensTeenBooks.com

HoodFamilyBlog.com
HoodFamily.com

www.ingramcontent.com/pod-product-compliance
Lightning Source LLC
Chambersburg PA
CBHW031235090426
42742CB00007B/209